Focus Your Way To Freedom

FOCUS YOUR WAY TO FREEDOM

Do property deals & travel the world
without getting stressed or working all the time

Jackie
Tomes

ISBN: 978-1-0686596-0-7

For my Mum & Dad – for always supporting and encouraging me to achieve my dreams, and letting me know that it would be ok even if I failed along the way.

Aim for the stars, but know that it will be ok

even if you hit the lamp-post on the way up.

Contents

Foreword

In 2019, I met up with Jackie at the Wellcome Café on Euston Road in London. Whilst we'd known each other since 2015, we hadn't seen each other for a few years, and it was great to catch up.

Jackie has a unique and brilliant way of spotting opportunities to improve things - her life, her business, the lives of others. Having spent almost two decades coaching and mentoring 1000s of business owners across multiple industries, I feel confident in saying that this is one of her greatest gifts to the world, a driving purpose in her life and what makes her such an inspirational leader. During the conversation, I was discussing the work I had been doing coaching other property business owners, and she lit up.

Jackie realised that the work I do around wellbeing, positive mindset and personal growth, and what she does with her business partner, Dave, would complement each other perfectly. So the discussion began in earnest. If I could coach her mentees, the business would become more holistic, providing mentees with greater certainty of success.

Less than a year later, I was facilitating alongside her and Dave at their Property Strategy Retreat in Margate. It was the start of a partnership between the three of us that has led to those that we work with achieving phenomenal results, not just in their business, but most importantly in their lives. Everyone is out there looking to raise more finance so that they can do more deals and hit their cashflow goals, but Jackie is the only person I know enabling people to do this and have more fun and happiness while they're at it! This approach is at the core of the business we run together, Property Strategy, and it has spawned a top 10 charting podcast and led to this book being written.

As we began working together we each focused on bringing our own unique area of expertise to our clients. Dave is the numbers guy, with a mind for detail and financial analysis – he's known as 'Detail Dave'. I am the mindset man, helping people to overcome their personal blockages and help them to perform at their peak to enable them to grow quicker. But Jackie really is the magic dust that allows us all to sparkle and thrive. She is the spearhead that drives us all forwards with her energy and focus, whilst also being the visionary that can see the bigger picture of where we are going. It is business leaders like Jackie that make the seemingly impossible, possible. But with Jackie there is another layer altogether, as she is somehow able to transfer that same visionary magic and tenacious drive to everyone she works with, inspiring others to achieve what they never believed they could.

It is amazing to be involved with so many people who are successfully investing in property, and aiming for the financial freedom that will allow them to live life on their own terms. It is fascinating to see how each person has different challenges and evolves through them in their own unique way. However, there is one challenge that everyone we work with must overcome – this is the one thing which is the same across all property investors (and indeed all business owners) who are looking to achieve financial freedom... That is managing the sheer volume of tasks on the to do list, the multitude of plates that need to be kept spinning, and the immense pressure that comes from constantly pushing yourself out of your comfort zone. At the toughest moments, this all manifests as overwhelm and stress, as an awful feeling of being weighed down by the pressure of it all.

The problem is that this so often means that we aren't enjoying the journey to creating our dream life. In fact, most of us end up proactively putting off happiness, telling ourselves "I'll be happy when I've..."

- Got the next deal completed (or 10, 20, 50 deals done!)
- Got this refinance over the line and paid that investor back

- Completed this refurb and got the property tenanted
- Quit my job
- Got £5k / £10k / £20k a month of passive income

The list goes on! Happiness is always just out of reach, somewhere in the future, rarely in the present, and our physical and mental health can suffer. The truth is that most stress comes from our immediate environment, yet we rarely take action to improve it.

However, in reading Jackie's account of her journey, you will get a rare glimpse into the mind and methods of someone who has not only managed to overcome the challenges blocking her way to freedom, but has worked out how to do it in a way that enables happiness and enjoyment along the way!

I am so excited for the release of this book – there are plenty of books on investing in property out there but there aren't books that bring together this full holistic picture of how to invest in property in a way that brings you true freedom, in all its forms.

This book will take you through the biggest lessons Jackie has learned in her search for Freedom in a way that I anticipate will have you searching your own soul in a bid to follow in her footsteps.

I hope you enjoy and learn as much from the insights in this book as I have through this partnership.

- Dominic Beecheno

Introduction

Whether you're just starting to explore property investing or you've already done several deals, this book will open your eyes to the industry, and your mind to a new way of thinking.

It's likely that you picked up this book because you desire financial freedom and you believe investing in property can get you there. However, if you've done more than a few deals, then harsh reality has already hit. Every new deal you do adds another layer of problems. Time-consuming and energy-sucking details just keep adding up. Instead of freedom, you've managed to create another job for yourself! That was NOT the plan.

You know some property investors who are 'living the life', driving nice cars, wearing nice clothes, and going on expensive holidays. And you know there are deals out there that can get you there too. But right now, you can't see how you can do enough deals without getting totally overwhelmed along the way.

You are not alone. Through mentoring hundreds of property investors, I've come to realise that we all face similar obstacles and challenges. Having been there and come out the other side, I know the feelings of frustration, overwhelm, and anxiety. I see myself in other people in property and I know how sh***y it can be sometimes.

I also know the feelings of triumph and joy that come with achieving the dream. The irony is that financial freedom isn't enough.

That's right, you read that correctly.... Financial freedom is NOT enough. But don't worry; whilst that might sound like a massive 'bubble burst'... it's actually good news, if you'll just stick with me, and hear me out.

This book is a true-to-life, tell-all story about how to gain true freedom through property investing. However, to do so means finally exposing the **Financial Freedom Fallacy** — the false belief that financial freedom is the answer to all life's problems.

We've all heard the adage "money can't buy you happiness". Intellectually, we know this to be true. Yet, nearly every entrepreneur, business owner, and property investor I've ever met or worked with starts with that one desire. If financial freedom through property investing is your goal, this book can help you get there — but make no mistake, it goes much deeper.

I wrote *Focus Your Way to Freedom* to help you avoid the pitfalls and to speed up your progress. But the book reveals dark moments, obstacles that other property experts attempt to hide, and the BS that the industry avoids talking about. It finally slays the dragon — the Financial Freedom Fallacy — that only serves to hold people back from ultimate freedom.

This is my story and the story of Tomes Homes — how it started, how we evolved, and the learnings along the way. I wish there had been someone who was transparent about how the property industry really works when I got started. We'd be where we are now, but within 5 years instead of 10. More importantly, we would have been happier and freer along the way.

It's been over 10 years since I decided to start Tomes Homes in 2013, with the first buy-to-let property completing in July 2014 for £108,500. When I started this crazy thing, I was working full-time in market research in London and just wishing that I could have more freedom (let's face it, there's never enough annual leave allowance!). I didn't want to have to ask permission to go on holiday. That, to me, is what freedom meant back then. But that mindset was before I learned all the lessons contained in this book.

Fast forward 10 years to 2023...

We spent the summer traveling around Europe in a motorhome living the MoHo lifestyle. It was wonderful...low stress...an absolute PLEASURE! Meanwhile, our business was ticking over. Whilst visiting Spain, we got the latest valuation on a big project and it was the BEST EVER! It had been an incredibly challenging project that took a huge amount of time and energy across the team. Like so often happens in property, many things had not gone to plan along the way. BUT we must have been doing something right because the £2.84M valuation (against a purchase price of £1.4M and refurb costs of around £450k) was £290k MORE than our most recent analysis had estimated! That's a pretty beautiful number, isn't it?

It ended up valued at £800K more than our original estimate when we agreed the deal two years earlier. Although we did end up spending a lot more in refurb than the original plan and experienced a lot of headaches during planning and execution, the extra effort we put into the property was well worth it in the end. So, cheers to THAT! We were absolutely delighted to report this back to our lovely Joint Venture partners and investors. On to the next project.

That's where Tomes Homes is now, 10 years on. £17M+ deals done, £7M+ private finance raised. Thanks to the systemised approach to doing deals that we've developed along the way, we've also been able to create a life where we can go on holiday every six weeks whilst this has been happening.

Out of all the painful lessons and successes we've had with Tomes Homes, we started Property Strategy where we've created and implemented strategies for £150M+ of other property investment businesses, helping them to raise finance and do more property deals in a way that creates FREEDOM. In 2023 we also launched our Top 10 Charting podcast, Property Lifestyle Mastery.

We've achieved a fair amount and we're very pleased with how far we've come. Still, it hasn't always been easy. For a long time, I didn't even come close to experiencing true freedom. In some ways, I wasn't even sure what that meant! There were a lot of very, very dark moments along the way.

At first we thought it was financial freedom that we needed. (We, too, fell for the Financial Freedom Fallacy!) It turns out that financial freedom is not enough — there's also a time freedom element. But it turns out that mastering time is still not enough. There's a third element — and it's only once you bring these three things together, through focus, that you start to hack true freedom.

That's what this book is about — the lessons underneath these three different areas of freedom. And how you must FOCUS to make them a reality. When I set out to write it, I didn't want it to be just another property book teaching various ways to invest, raise finance, structure deals, and build a property portfolio.

I will share with you, by telling my story, how I made mistakes that cost time and money and health, so you don't have to make those mistakes. Or, if you do (because, let's face it, sometimes mistakes get made), you'll recognise them sooner and learn the lessons faster.

We have been chasing freedom for over 10 years and this book is a way to consolidate, share, and pass on the sometimes-painful learnings that we've had along the way. Maybe after reading this you won't totally avoid all the road humps coming your way, but you'll catch yourself sooner to be able to speed your way through those tough moments when they happen.

The property training industry happily sells the idea that anyone can do it. All you have to do is "take MASSIVE action", say "YES" to opportunities, follow a "simple system", and escape the 9-to-5 in a few years' time. So off you go, in search of property deals to match what you read about in books or hear from stages. BUT as I'm sure you are starting to realise, nothing is ever as cut-and-dried as the marketing hype makes it out to be.

You deserve freedom, and this book is the perfect start to getting you on track. Take a step back, shut out the noise, and get ready to Focus Your Way to Freedom.

A note about the book's structure:

The bulk of *Focus Your Way to Freedom* is my story. I've bared my soul so you get a clear idea of the kinds of things that happen in this industry and the challenges you may face.

At the end of some chapters you will find **Freedom Formulas** — the biggest lessons I've gathered from my experience. These formulas are there to help you grow your property business in a better way for a stress-free (or at least lower stress) outcome.

Also, peppered throughout the book you will encounter **Recipes for Freedom**. These are very brief tactical shortcuts that can help you simplify your property business, get clear on priorities, and learn to focus better.

There is a **Resources** page at the back of the book. There you'll find access to some of our free resources to help you take forward the learnings from this book and put them into action. If you're keen to check out these resources as you read, you will find them here:

www.property-strategy.com/focus

If you are not interested in the Freedom Formulas, Recipes for Freedom or our Resources, that's perfectly fine. You can skip those sections and simply enjoy the story.

Lastly, I do talk a lot about 'Business Models' during this book so I just wanted to clarify what I mean by this before we dive in. The property industry refers to HMOs, single-lets, commercial conversions, rent-to-rent, developments, etc... as 'Property Strategies'. But I think this is a very unhelpful term – I think we should refer to them as 'Business Models'.

What's the difference? Well, a business model describes what the business actually does.

In the beginning, I was *doing* buy-to-let and *doing* it on a buy, refurbish, refinance basis. Therefore, that was my business model – Buy, Refurbish, Refinance BTL flats. So, first choose your model.

Then start asking yourself *how* am a going to BUILD this business around that model? Strategy is everything that fits around your business model — all the moving parts in the business that keep the business doing what it does and ensuring it achieves its larger goals. It includes all the aspects that will enable you to achieve the freedom you desire such as pipeline processes, systems, financial management, team planning, and so much more.

This is why I like to make this distinction, because for example, doing Commercial Conversions is not a strategy in itself, and without a proper strategy, you'll really struggle to make sure you are doing Commercial Conversions in a way that helps you to achieve YOUR bigger goals.

To more deals, more cashflow and most importantly... to freedom!

Jackie x

Part One

Chapter 1

The Chicken Jointing Mindset

In 2013, I was working full-time in market research in Covent Garden. I had a week of annual leave planned. You know when you're working full-time like that? You *really* look forward to your precious holiday days. It's a BIG moment in the calendar, right? You plan it all out — it's a massive deal.

That year, my partner Dave and I went to Courchevel La Tania in the French Alps. You'll get to know Dave, now my husband and business partner, throughout this book. At the time, we'd been together for 10 years. Yes, we were teenage sweethearts! But we'd never skied together, so this was our first skiing holiday.

It was a magical week. The brochures describe La Tania as 'an unspoiled corner of paradise'. And it *was* paradise. Our apartment was tiny but perfect The snow was amazing. The skies blue. And, to top it off, towards the end of the week was my 24th birthday! On the slopes! Glorious.

I was up early on my birthday, sitting on the sofa, taking in the peace outside our rented apartment. It was beautiful as the sun started to rise. It had been an AMAZING holiday, but a feeling of unease bubbled below the surface. You know that dull, sinking feeling you start to get in the pit of your stomach as a holiday comes to an end? It's the 'Sunday night' feeling, but times ten! You're trying to prepare yourself to go back to work on

Monday. Dread creeps in and you don't want to go back... but you know you must.

That was me. Then it hit me: Not only did I not want to go back to work on Monday, I DESPERATELY did not want to go back to work on Monday! As this realisation sunk in, it's like my heart in my chest started to get pulled down into the sinkhole that was opening up in the pit of my stomach. And it was as if my brain was swooping in trying to help me with the thought of a beautiful daydream...

Imagine... imagine how good it would be to say 'F— this, let's just stay for another week!'

Oh my days, could you imagine?! What if! What if... I could just stay here for as long as I wanted. What if I didn't have to beg for anyone's permission to stay. It was the sweetest daydream, that sparkled in my mind as the sun's rays started to fill the slope in front of me, making the snow sparkle like millions of tiny crystals. It was a wonderful DREAM...But HOW?!

I knew there must be some way. I believed anything was possible with enough hard work and tenacity. I'd always loved the idea of having my own business, but I'd never had any good enough ideas... I knew property was a possibility, so my daydream now shifted this way. I'd seen my mum and stepdad buy, renovate, and then sell a couple of properties. I'd also bought my own flat during the 2009 property slump which had made me the easiest £60k of my life in just 4 years of owning it. Maybe there's something in this property thing?! I hit the mobile data roaming bill hard and downloaded four books on property investing from Amazon. Happy Birthday to me!

That was a moment of decision for me. In that moment on 25 January 2013, everything changed. It was key for many reasons that will become clear as you read this book. For now, it's enough to know that an idea turned into a dream and dread turned into determination.

I told myself:

Life is going to change. I don't know exactly how, but at some point in the future I'm going to be here in La Tania again. And maybe if I feel this feeling of dread, of not wanting to go back to work, I'll be able to do something about it and STAY. Stay here skiing in the mountains for as many WEEKS as my heart desires.

And so, the adventure began...

It was 18 months from that moment of decision until I bought my first investment property. To do it, I had to make sacrifices, so let's just say they were 18 of the most socially boring months of my life!

I contacted all my friends and said "Hey, I love you guys, but I'm not going to be going out with you for a while. I've GOT to buy a property. To buy a property, I've got to save up for the deposit, and to do that I've got to stop spending on **anything** except the actual essentials."

My initial plan was that with a second job, and five to ten disciplined years, I could have a small property portfolio generating a few thousand per month and not have to work for anyone else. Then I wouldn't have to ask for permission to go on holiday (even if they wouldn't be luxury holidays).

Dave says that's when I 'really got my money management head on'. It was clear to me that I needed to change the way I thought about money. I looked at all my costs and asked *what can I get rid of?* I didn't look at property investment and just think *I need to make this much money.* I first thought *what can I cut?* so that the number to quit my job was as low as possible (not just about replacing my salary), and also so I could start SAVING hard for the first deposit.

It was all done in a very logical, rational manner because I was serious about 'escaping the rat race' in the shortest time possible. Since I didn't have the funds to get into property, I started by creating the first draft of what has subsequently been named my Finances of Life spreadsheet.

Finances of Life

I created the Finances of Life spreadsheet by going through my bank statements for the previous 12 months, listing every expense category. Anything I spent money on, like car insurance, home insurance, travel — you get the idea.

Then I created two columns: CURRENT and POTENTIAL. The CURRENT column had all my expenses as they stood at that moment —

right down to food shopping and haircuts. At the very bottom I had that killer row called LEFT FOR SAVING.

Moving over to the POTENTIAL column, I got ruthless. How much money did I *really* need to spend to live my life?! What was the bare minimum required to get by so that the LEFT FOR SAVING amount could be as high as possible? The weekly shop became a game. How little could I spend?!

Jamie Oliver Helped Me Buy My First Property

It's true! *Save with Jamie*[1] became my food bible! It added fuel to the fire that culminated one day when I learned the sacred art of chicken jointing! Why? Because it was the cheapest way to buy chicken! (See page 94 of Jamie's book to learn how to do it.)

For about a year, I bought only whole chickens. Then I'd joint them, use them in different recipes, and freeze what I wasn't using right away. This mindset — what I've come to call the Chicken Jointing Mindset — is one of the most important shifts you can make if you want to speed your route to financial freedom.

Alongside this, I built my savings with that second job. I started dying my hair at home and stopped buying new clothes. When my car got written off, I chose not to buy a new one as it wasn't essential. I swapped the train commute for a road bike and used the 25-mile round trip each day as training for a triathlon! Eventually, I realised I could get an interest-free credit card, do my day-to-day spending on it, and SAVE that money too. I squirreled away all my pennies towards a deposit for my first property like my life depended on it. But there's a lot more to property investing than just the deposit...

Saving Was the Easy Part

I started avidly reading the property books I'd downloaded from Amazon. I

1. Jamie Oliver (2013) *Save with Jamie: Shop Smart, Cook Clever, Waste Less* (London: Penguin Books Ltd.) 94

then started looking at areas where I might potentially invest. We were based in South East London at the time, in a place called West Thamesmead near Woolwich Arsenal. Based on what I read in the property books, I started looking for potential properties in the areas around us.

There were a lot of one bed and studio flats in Erith selling for around £80k. When I looked at the rents on these properties, I realised there was a sweet spot in terms of the property values versus rental yield. That got me very excited and because I'd gotten so good at saving, I knew it was only a matter of time before I had enough money for the first deposit.

At this point, I started googling mortgage brokers for contact numbers. I then started to make phone calls and have meetings. I even went into the bank where I had my current account, just to see if they'd give me a mortgage. It was brutal; they literally laughed in my face!

The mortgage brokers weren't much better. When I told them I was trying to get as high a loan-to-value as possible, they laughed. They said it was impossible and that I was never going to do it. I had to speak to five or six mortgage brokers before I found one that would take me seriously and give me the time of day.

At the same time, I was also reading *Your Property Network* (YPN) magazine on the tube during my journeys to and from work. Every month I would read the mortgage update published in YPN by Stuart Yardley. I saw there was one lender with a mortgage product that only required a 15% deposit! Whoa, gamechanger! Suddenly the 'magic number' to get the first property dropped substantially and I could see my path to saving enough to buy one of these £80k properties. So in the late summer or early autumn of 2013, I applied for a mortgage.

Declined

The one lender who would do something for a 15% deposit declined me because I was only 24! They actually said that I must be 25 to get this mortgage because CLEARLY that's when I'd be mature enough to handle a buy-to-let mortgage?! That put our whole journey back a good three to six months.

To make matters worse, when I turned 25 and was finally 'mature enough' to qualify for a mortgage, the market had started to shift. I went to Erith again to look at properties, and those I could previously find online for around £80k were now selling for upwards of £100k. Of course, my reaction was *wow, this is a really bad deal now, Erith doesn't work any more.* And so began a wild goose chase, looking for properties in other areas.

Starting in Erith, I worked my way out towards the Kent coast bit by bit. From Dartford, to Gravesend, Chatham and Gillingham, eventually ending up in Dover! For each location, I researched the area, went on viewings, and started to put in offers. Every time an offer got rejected, I tried to figure out why. I was learning how to analyse a deal and it was during this time that we created our first rudimentary deal analyser.

It was hard; it was a really hot market and it was difficult fitting viewings into my life whilst working full time and doing research. In the evenings after work, I'd get the train out of Central London to somewhere in deep, dark Kent only to view grotty properties, get messed around by agents, get played off against other investors in an attempt to get me to raise my offers... It was not a very enjoyable part of the process.

It took a good three to six months of this before I finally got an offer accepted on a house out in Dover. But just after my offer was accepted, I decided to look at Erith again from a different perspective. I couldn't get a one bed or studio flat for £80k anymore — by that time they were selling for around £110k. But did that mean it was a bad deal?

When I started to look at it with this new perspective, it dawned on me that even though prices had gone up, the numbers still worked. So I pulled out of the deal in Dover and started looking in Erith again, with far greater focus on finding properties that fitted my price bracket and criteria. I went for it, and that is how I subsequently agreed and bought the very first investment property.

25 July 2014

This was the day my first deal completed. It had taken 18 months of blood, sweat, and saving, but I'd done it! I bought my first investment property for

£108,500 with a 15% deposit (85% LTV mortgage). The only thing left to do was refurb, get it let, and re-mortgage.

Obviously, money was still tight. I was self-funding the entire project, scraping everything together, so I was very keen to be cost-effective with the refurb. Being new to property, I had to figure out what I could do myself and what required a builder. I did a lot of research, trying to find the best price for a kitchen. Eventually, I found a refurb contractor who agreed to do the kitchen and bathroom. The rest of it we would, as much as possible, do ourselves. So on the day we completed, I took a day of annual leave and went to the property to do the rubbish clearance myself.

It. Was. Disgusting!

It was like the flat had never been cleaned since it was built in the '80s. The carpets were disgusting, it smelled of smoked, in fact it stank... It was NOT a nice property but I was trying to save money. So I pulled up the nasty carpets, took stuff to the tip myself, and did everything possible to scrimp and save on that first refurb.

Another big challenge on the first refurb project was getting used to working with a contractor. I had to figure out which problems the contractor could solve, and which came back to me. For example, the water pressure wasn't strong enough to make the shower work, so we needed to install a new water pump. When I asked the refurb contractor about it, he informed me that he couldn't advise on that and that I would need to go to an electrician.

When it turned out that a new pump was going to cost £150, I was in tears. It was a whole palaver — I hadn't budgeted for a water pump, I didn't know how to fix it, and at the time it seemed like a massive problem. Looking back, it almost seems ridiculous but I was doing everything on a shoestring budget and learning at the same time.

It was an intense period, juggling the refurb, managing the refurb contractor, ordering materials, even fitting door handles and lights... all whilst still doing a full-time job. We were on site evenings and weekends and it became all-consuming. But after a stressful month juggling work and the refurb, a lovely teaching assistant moved in as my first tenant.

Six months later, we refinanced. Below are the numbers for my first deal. If you are an experienced property investor, the numbers might look small. I was ridiculously disappointed with the pretty minor £7,500 down valuation when we re-mortgaged, but a win is a win and I'm proud of that first property!

Purchase Price	£108,500
Purchase Costs	£3,000
Refurb	£7,500
Total Costs	£119,000
Cash Required: (85% LTV Mortgage)	£26,775
End Value: (Downval from 132,500)	£125,000
Project Profit	£6,000
Cash Left In	£14,025
Ongoing Cashflow (per Calendar Month)	**£225**
ROI on money left in	19%

My First Ever Deal Numbers

Excel spreadsheets, discipline, and jointing chickens had WORKED! But actually this process did SO MUCH MORE for me than just getting me to that first investment property. It got me living WELL WITHIN my means. Developing the Chicken Jointing Mindset gave me a sense of control over my future. By the time we'd bought enough properties to replace income from my job, I was confident in my ability to manage finances and grow our property business. This, in turn, empowered me to hand in my notice much sooner than I would otherwise have been able to. Which meant I created the time and energy to build more!

Freedom Formula:
Control Overheads to Maximise Cashflow

I didn't just think *'I want to buy property'* — I was determined. I didn't just say *'I want to fire my boss'* — I made a decision. And I didn't just want to track my expenses — I wanted financial freedom. So it wasn't only cutting out new clothes, not getting my nails done, or not going out with friends. I went all in and looked at every expense.

The Chicken Jointing Mindset showed me how living with LESS in the SHORT-TERM can give you SO MUCH MORE in the mid-to-long-term. So if you are wondering how to move ahead in property from a standing start, here are a few key thoughts from someone who's been where you are:

1. **Don't be afraid to cut back to move forward.** I know you may be getting into property because you want to have a more opulent life, but sometimes you have to have LESS NOW to have MORE SOONER.
2. **Manage your money!** Don't bury your head in the sand — this knowledge will give you power and control over your life. Be harsh with yourself — do you really need those new shoes, that gym-membership, or to buy lunch at work each day? I'll give you a clue... NO! Resole your old shoes, go for a run instead, make a sandwich!
3. **You CAN'T have it ALL NOW.** You have to prioritise what you want. If your ultimate goal is to live a life of FREEDOM, then it's going to be a tough few years building to get there. But, as someone who has gone from jointing her own chickens and saving pennies to £17M+ deals done and complete financial freedom in 10 years, I promise you that if you do this with ruthless focus you can get there! You CAN have everything you want sooner than you could imagine.

Learn to maximise cashflow by controlling your overheads. Develop the Chicken Jointing Mindset and apply it to your life and property business. Once learnt and implemented, it will speed up your route to financial freedom.

Recipes for Freedom

It's nothing fancy, but my Finances of Life spreadsheet is a great way to get started. You can find it, along with the other resources mentioned in this book, at: www.property-strategy.com/focus

Make it fun. You might be surprised at how much you're spending on unnecessary things!

Chapter 2

Chasing Shiny Pennies

After we 'closed the door' on the first refurbishment I can remember driving away with Dave, full of excitement and possibility, and remarking to him (almost as a side comment!), "I think we could do more than one of these in a year...". WELL, Dave almost crashed the car in horror. That first property had drained us as we juggled everything around full-time jobs. Dave was not at all on board with the idea. But inside my head, I continued to scheme...

How could I earn more money to be able to save more? Or were there further savings I could make? I reckoned I could double down and make it happen. Even if the next five years quite literally disappeared into a sea of hard work and saving, the snow-covered mountains were calling and I wanted to be able to answer!

Up until this point I'd only ever read books, I hadn't done any property training courses. But in the autumn of 2014, I attended my first course (dragging an unwilling Dave along behind me) — Multiple Streams of Property Income with Progressive Property. The possibilities put forward by the inspirational Rob Moore absolutely blew my mind. Particularly when it came to working with other peoples' money and raising finance to grow quicker.

I'd heard it mentioned in books and had occasionally thought about the idea. But if I'm honest, I just didn't believe anyone would want to invest in me. What did I have to offer? I had just kept pushing the idea to one side.

Like a bucket of cold water being thrown in your face, I suddenly had a very rude wake-up call... Whilst jointing chickens had gotten me here, if I kept thinking like this it would HOLD me here! Rather than being a stingy penny-pincher, it was time to change my mindset around what 'investing' really is. For me that meant paying good money to educate myself on how to be a professional investor and learn how to raise finance, because if I could solve that riddle, I would remove the biggest barrier to doing more deals! I could do as many deals as I wanted if I wasn't held back by how quickly I could save up.

It was also a very important moment because that was when Dave came around to a bigger vision of what we could achieve through property in a very short timeframe if we could figure out how to raise finance. It shifted from property investing being 'my thing' (with him as a cheerleader), to 'our' thing. This was such an important decision – with Dave alongside me I just knew it would transform what was possible. He's always blown me away with how smart he is - no matter how complicated a problem he could always seem to find a way through. He was also incredible at maths and numbers, so I knew he could really make the analysis and numbers side of the business so much better. I'd seen how well the partnership between Rob Moore and Mark Homer had worked for Progressive Property. Rob was the visionary for the business and clearly incredibly skilled at marketing and positioning the business; whereas Mark was very detail orientated and excellent at taking care of the operational side of the business. I had the feeling that Dave had the potential to be the 'Mark Homer' for Tomes Homes!

It was time to start buying chicken like normal people again and use my money to invest in training courses and mentorship. That way I could leverage the expertise of those who knew more than me; in particular, how to work with investors. It was time to start thinking like an investor, not a saver.

This shift in mindset shot us off into the next phase like a rocket ship! I remember posting on social media regularly, updating my friends and family when the next offer had been accepted. "Offer number 2 accepted", "3rd Tomes Home in the bag". My colleagues in the office went from being incredibly proud that I'd bought the first investment property, to completely bemused when it kept on happening.

The focused approach to do more buy-refurbish-refinance, buy-to-let deals was a 'strategic accident'. I had no idea how important it would turn out to be. But thanks to that focus, it was straightforward to present a plan for doing a number of these kinds of deals because we already had the 'know-how' and 'the numbers' to back it up. Thanks to this, over the next 12 months or so, we completed on another 10 deals.

However, the more I attended property industry networking events and training courses, the more I became aware of all these other opportunities I hadn't seen before. So of course, instead of sticking to the same business model that had been working well for us, we decided what everyone else was doing MUST be better.

And that is how I started down one of the most hideous paths any property investor could take, fuelled by one of the biggest lies in the industry. A path that set us back months— if not years — because what everyone else was doing sounded...

So Sexy & So Cool

I started to look at the buy-to-let model I was doing compared to HMOs, and I wondered *am I doing this all wrong? Why go to all this effort, taking six months to buy, refurb, and get the property tenanted for a measly £225 per month?*

We had been quite happy with our £225 per month at that time. But when I looked at the potential to earn £1,000 per month from just one property, suddenly I didn't feel so good about it. Then I met people doing rent-to-rent. I had not heard of rent-to-rent back in 2014. OMG!

These guys were doing HMOs, but they didn't even have to buy the property, Instead, they rented it from the current owner as a single let and then rented it out to five or six people and pocketed the margin. These guys were generating £1,000-plus per month on properties they didn't even own! And achieving it in under 30-days!! The idea that you could make money from a property that you don't even own, with ongoing cash-flow... It totally BLEW MY MIND! And it made me seriously re-evaluate all the work we had to do for single lets with just £225 cash-flow each.

It made me question again — *is it really worth it?*

As I carried on going to events, I met new people doing serviced accommodation, flips, title-splits, and developments. I will NEVER FORGET that first event where I met a guy who I thought, at that time, was the coolest, frickin' dude I had ever met.

"Jackie, love, I do commercial to residential conversions. I don't get out of bed for less than £500k on a deal."

JAW. DROP.

£500,000?! Per deal!! I wanted to do deals like THAT! I started questioning what I was doing. Suddenly, the small profit I'd made on my first property investment seemed even worse than I thought! I had started hearing at networking events that doing commercial conversions weren't even that much harder than simple refurbs and buy-to-lets. "Just add a zero or two", they said.

I started thinking...

Maybe I need to be doing some of these different "strategies"? Maybe some rent-to-rent HMO"s for quicker cash-flow; some HMOs to maximise return on investment. Maybe some commercial conversions or developments to make some big pots of cash.

I only want to get out of bed for more than £500k profit on a deal, I thought...

Before I knew it, what started out as a very focused strategy suddenly went really wide. Still, I was lucky that my initial burst of focus had lasted long enough to get a portfolio of single lets agreed before the shiny penny monster really got his claws into me!

However, there was one thing I kept hearing at the networking events I attended that just made these shiny pennies seem even more urgent. In hindsight it turned out to be some of the worst advice in the industry — and we fell for it. Hook, line, and sinker...

The Biggest Lie in Property

"You should diversify to reduce your risk."

You hear a lot about diversification in relation to financial investments, and the property industry is no different. Thinking about stocks and shares as an example, it means not putting all your money into one company or one fund. Spreading your investments over a number of global stocks and funds assures you aren't overexposed to one business, industry, or country. It means you're protected should there be an unexpected drop in one area. It makes a lot of sense.

In property, diversification tends to mean investing in multiple different business models, such as Single Lets, HMOs, and Commercial Conversions. It is suggested as a way to lower risk so you aren't over-exposed to one area or tenant type. It increases your different types of income so it's not all coming from the same source. On the surface it seems to make a lot of sense as a way of mitigating risk, right?

However, there is one big difference between financial investments and property investing, which the industry does not seem to talk about. Financial investments are a form of passive investment, where you invest in other businesses or assets around the globe. Being a Property Investor, meaning you are the one finding deals and raising funds, is a business in its own right. You are the one running the business, not passively investing in someone else's. It's like comparing an investment into the FTSE 100, which requires a few clicks of your mouse, to setting up and running your own restaurant, which is a full-time job as an entrepreneur! It is not the same thing.

When it comes to diversifying in property, starting up a new business model is a bit like a restaurateur choosing to start up a shoe shop next to their restaurant. These businesses are only similar in that each sells a product from a shop front, but everything else is completely different. Different product, different clients, different marketing, different sales methods, different processes... you get the picture.

Diversifying across two different business models in property is more like setting up two businesses at the same time. Something that few people would consider a sane thing to do if they really thought about it.

Our business model — single lets that generated £200-£300 pounds per month (after allowances for voids and maintenance), took 6-12 months to buy, refurbish, get cash-flowing, and re-mortgage — had started to seem boring.

Put that together with the shiny penny, grass-is-greener issue of seeing what others were doing — all those SEXY and COOL deals — and it sent me on a downward spiral from being super focused on one business model, to a big time "Fear of Missing Out" (FOMO).

I hadn't yet clocked the learning that I've just shared, that each business model was like its own little business. I had started to think that we should be doing more, more, more. "Dave, we've got to DIVERSIFY!" I would command.

This diversification was heavily fuelled by relentless comparison to what everyone else was doing in property — there was always someone else doing something better than I was! This was shiny penny syndrome in full force, and before I knew it, the focus we'd had when we started was suddenly out the window. And it wasn't just single lets, HMOs, and commercial conversions. We ended up looking at title splits, developments, packaging up deals and flips — we had seven different models we were pursuing at our most distracted point.

There I was, pursuing multiple strategies based on the rationalisation that 'diversification is good'.

And it didn't even stop there...

Shiny Pennies and Impostor Syndrome

It wasn't just pursuing multiple business models that split my focus. I had found that it was much easier to attract interest from potential investors if you were the one on stage speaking at networking events. So that's what I started doing, using my success so far to give me something to talk about on stage — which is how I first met the lovely Jayne Owen who was part of the *Your Property Network* (YPN) magazine team.

Here's what Jayne said to me:

"Jackie, I love your story. You've gone from taking 18 months to buy one property, to buying another 10 in the next 12 months. That's an amazing story! People would want to hear about that!"

That resulted in our first feature in *Your Property Network* magazine in 2015. Suddenly, what I was doing was elevated. And from that platform, I realised that I actually had knowledge and skills that could help others to succeed in property, which started me down the path of mentoring. Another stream of income so, therefore, another way to diversify and reduce risk, right? And just like that, my mentorship and consultancy business Property Strategy was born.

So with seven exciting business models, regular speeches around the property networking event circuit, and my mentoring beginning to take off, it all started to look really, really good... at least from the outside. But underneath, all was not well.

You see there was a major difference between how the property industry perceived us and the success we were having, versus how I felt about our property business. I felt in conflict — incongruent — because with all those business models, mentoring, training, and speeches, I was totally overwhelmed. Everything just felt chaotic, and with all these distractions pulling me in every direction, I was now struggling to secure new deals! It felt like I was living off past success, and how everyone perceived us now was not how it felt inside. And that started to make me feel just a little bit uncomfortable. I was experiencing impostor syndrome and it made me start to fancy one of the most raved about shiny pennies in the industry - the one I'd been salivating about since I met that cool dude at the property networking event who didn't get out of bed for less than £500k profit on a deal...

We'd heard that it was no harder to do these massive commercial conversions than it was doing a refurb... Just BIGGER NUMBERS and bigger profits! And I thought to myself *well, if that's the case, surely this has to be the answer — more money from less deals, therefore less work, and a model that will elevate my image and make me FEEL successful.*

Alongside the mentoring and the speeches, this felt like the simplest way to reduce the overwhelm and get rid of the imposter syndrome that was bubbling away inside. Of course, I would still carry on looking for single lets and HMOs because I'd already done the hard work of learning how to do them, and I believed they were a **good diversification** that would help solve my immediate desire to increase our monthly cashflow. It was a great rationalisation for the creator in me to say...

Let's do loads of stuff. It's reducing my risk!

The 10X Fallacy

In the end, the result of shiny penny syndrome was that we managed to **10X our WORKLOAD, but NOT our cash flow!**

We were working longer hours. I was still juggling all these property projects around my full-time job, going to networking events, meeting investors, learning new things. We had refurbs going on. Meanwhile, Dave was working as a musician. We were working seven days a week, 18 hours a day. It was crazy!

Imagine your mind is spinning with buy-to-let, rent-to-rent, deal packaging, serviced accommodation, HMOs, commercial conversions, development... and you want to say YES to all of it! It's human nature. We all want a reason to do something new and exciting.

The problem is, you don't realise the limits of your capabilities because you're so wired. The adrenaline is pumping and you just keep pushing and pushing. I pushed so hard that I wasn't willing to listen to all the signs of burnout. The more you say yes, the more confused, overwhelmed, time-poor, and further from your goals you end up feeling. Sometimes it felt just SO EXCITING, but at other times I was just EXHAUSTED. So, you push more. Drink more coffee to get through the tiredness... but eventually, the body will just MAKE you LISTEN.

Tears

I remember attending one of my monthly mentorship training days on the Progressive Property VIP Programme, and as usual I was pulling my suitcase along behind because I hadn't been home in a few days – I was totally exhausted. There were dark circles under my eyes that I'd tried to hide under my make-up, and I was doing my best to put a calm and positive face on top of what felt so shaky and uncertain underneath. Another member and friend, Glenn Delve, who was a great support at that time, approached me with open arms and a big smile, "Jackie! Lovely to see you. How's it going?!"

I don't even know where it came from, but my answer was streaming tears! It was like someone asking how I was doing just made me snap. I was overwhelmed, out of my comfort zone, trying to juggle all these different things. Worse, the money was just going out, and not coming back in yet, and I felt like I was supposed to come to these events and keep up the façade that everything was going great and I was loving my new life — because that's how everyone else I spoke to came across.

Imagine, you're pouring time and energy and resources into all these deals, but you're no f—— closer to financial freedom! You're just working really hard for no more financial rewards. That was the moment — it might have been April 2015 — that I started to crack. All I could think was *I'm not sure if we're doing the right thing.*

From the time we bought our first property to my first burnout took less than a year.

Dave and I see this often in property investors. It's one reason for this tell-all book. I've always been driven; push, push, PUSH! But we see it with everyone — it just happens in different ways. My way of hitting burnout was breaking down in tears after an extreme period and questioning everything I was doing.

We often see it with people who lack clarity and focus. Or they get a couple of projects going at the same time and managing everything is overwhelming. They realise *I can't do this* and break in a different way.

My story is just one example of what we've seen over-and-over again. The problem is you never really hear about it. Nobody wants to share this on social media — or be honest about it. I can't blame anyone for that. When you are at your lowest and most vulnerable, the last thing you want is to plaster it across social media. Which is why I'm telling you here. But don't worry, this book isn't just a warning. Later, I will also be sharing some of my favourite methods and options for avoiding burnout altogether.

Freedom Formula:
Focus, Focus, Focus

There's a lot of hype in the property industry around '10X THIS and 10X THAT'.

The reality was that, with distraction in full force, the rate at which we were able to secure deals slowed down massively.

If you do not focus on YOUR business model, you will get distracted. If you try to 'diversify to lower risk' at the wrong time, you'll only end up chasing shiny pennies — and missing the golden nuggets.

If you truly want to 10X your business, then start putting 10 times more focus and attention into the ONE THING that you want to get working for you. Put 10 times more effort into resolving the actual challenges you encounter (rather than thinking there must be another easier option out there), and put 10X more energy into setting everything up well from the beginning so that it can operate without you as quickly as possible. Then pretty soon you'll find that you are putting in smaller and smaller amounts of energy and time to keep the business running, and the effort-to-reward ratio turns on its head. 10 times *more* reward for 10 times less effort. That's how to truly become scalable and 10X your business.

My approach to building a successful property investment company is much more in-line with Andrew Carnegie (the American steel magnate and one of the richest Americans in history):

> "The way to become rich is to put all your eggs in one basket...
>
> and then watch that basket."

If you put all of your business eggs in one basket, and watch it like a hawk, you will have the time and headspace needed to be able to flex and adapt when things aren't working. This type of focus actually de-risks your business as you are able to react to challenges much more quickly.

Recipe for Freedom

Here's a simple concept that I've found very helpful for sidelining shiny pennies to stop them from slowing you down:

Whenever you find COOL or SEXY ideas that you want to try, simply write them down in a notebook, and call it your 'Ideas Bank'. That way you won't lose them. The opportunities will still be there later and there's no need to split your focus right now.

Chapter 3

Send Me Deals, I Want to Invest

Our initial investors were all family members, and it was a great experience working out how to do everything with people we already had a good dose of trust and unconditional love with. It meant that we didn't feel everything had to be perfect, and we just got on with the job of sharing with them that it would be worth investing with us. We used the first deal we'd done in 2014 as a case study to put forward the idea, and proposed buying more of the same type of properties (e.g., rundown, 1-bedroom flats) in the same area (the outskirts of South East London – Abbey Wood, Erith and Belvedere).

But eventually you've got to start finding people outside your family. At the raising finance training courses we'd done, I'd heard that you should go and basically 'hang out' at fancier places if you wanted to find people with money.

So I started looking for places in London that I could go and do that. I came across these weird things called private members clubs. I had never heard of them before and really didn't know what to expect. Just before your mind starts wondering, I don't mean strip clubs! Although maybe that would work too... (I'll leave that to your imagination.)

Networking and 'Easy' Money

Before discovering private members clubs, I was looking for expensive gyms, thinking that was the place to meet potential investors. But when I found members clubs, I realised they had their own gyms. They also had bars, restaurants, and networking events. I thought *this could be great.*

I started looking into different members clubs in London. For most of them, it's like breaking into a prison. It's really hard to get into them unless you know the right people, and at this point I definitely did not know the right people. You have to be proposed by a current member and then seconded by another member. You have to go through an interview process. Quite often, you have to demonstrate some level of financial means. The very same financial means we were trying to create, but we weren't there yet.

Eventually, I managed to find one private members club called Home House where you didn't have to be proposed and seconded. It was the only one I could find where it was just an interview to get in. So, I applied to Home House to try and get a membership.

This was during my 'Jackie spends no money on anything that's not essential' phase, so I was still being really careful with money at this point. It had been 18 months — maybe even two years — since I'd bought any new clothes. I hadn't been getting my hair done, hadn't been doing my nails. Basically, **I didn't look like I belonged in a private members club!**

So I went to TK Maxx and bought myself the most expensive looking cheap outfit that I could find to wear to my interview for Home House. The result? They let me in — GREAT! Now I just had to go out there and actually network, right? Getting in was the easy part, so I started prepping myself. Before I attended my first Home House business event, I practised my elevator pitch so it would sound natural:

Hi, I'm Jackie, I'm a property investor. I work with people who want to invest their money into property, but they don't have the time, knowledge or inclination to do so themselves.

So along I went to this networking event and started introducing myself to people using my little pitch. And it was only the first or second person that I met who asked the question I wanted to hear...

"All right, are you looking for investment at the moment?"

I'm thinking *be cool, be cool, be cool...*

"Yeah, we're always looking to talk to new potential partners."

His answer?

"I'd invest with you."

Of course, at that point I was both trying to play it cool whilst also feeling blown away by how easy this networking thing was!

"Yeah, I'd invest with you. I'd invest up to £2M."

To this point, the most we'd raised was around £150,000. Here was someone telling me he'd invest £2M! He continued...

"I'll invest £2M with you, as long as you can give me a first charge at 12% per annum return, and an exit within two years. Can you do that?"

Hopefully, you are asking the same question that was going through my mind at the time: *Could I do that?* To be honest, I had no clue. So I did what I thought was the right thing.

I said, "Yes."

I was sure we could figure out a way to do it. Then it really hit me and I got SO excited! You know when you have a ball of butterflies and energy inside, but you're also trying to be poker cool on the outside? That was me. I excused myself and went to the ladies' room and called Dave.

"Dave, it f—— worked! I've just talked to an investor who said he'd invest £2M with us!!"

Do you know what Dave said?

"What the f— are you doing in the toilet? Get back out there!"

Too funny, right? So I went back out there. We spent the rest of the evening talking. I was AMAZED at how easy it was to raise finance! At the end of the event, we swapped business cards. And that's when, as he was giving me his card, he said one of the most important sentences I'd heard but had no idea what it *really* meant...

"When you've got a deal, send it over..."

I remember being on the Tube headed home, cheesy pop music in my headphones, and it was like being in a movie. I'd nailed it. £2M!? That's it, I've done it! It's coming! I could almost feel the snowflakes that would be falling on me on all the skiing holidays I'd be booking VERY SOON.

When I got home, Dave and I opened our rudimentary 'deal analyser' to see if we could do what the investor wanted. Remember, I'd said 'yes' without actually knowing if it was possible? Can you guess what the actual answer was?

No.

Not on the single let flats we had been buying up until this point. We tried so many different ways, but one bed flats in South East London just could not do this. I'll cover more about why it wouldn't work in the next chapter, but for now, suffice it to say that it wasn't possible based on our existing business model. However, do you think I let that get in the way of a £2M investment? All we had to do was find the type of deal that would work, right?

What we did next set us back at least a year, if not longer, and brought with it a lot of lessons, the first of which was an important one called:

The 'Find the Deal' Fallacy

After realising we couldn't meet the investor's conditions with single lets, we started hunting for a deal that *would* work. As you know I was VERY excited to be looking at different 'strategies' so we could get onto 'diversifying'!

Eventually, after a lot of searching, viewings, research, phone calls and running numbers, we found something. A house that I thought we could convert into two flats. I remember it well because we spent an entire weekend figuring out how to put together a deal pack! On Sunday night, we sent it to him. Then, we waited for his response. And waited. And waited. And...

You get the idea. Tumbleweed. Nothing. No excited phone call. No email. No 'great deal, let's draw up the legal documents and get started'. No reply. Complete and utter silence. We were shocked. Based on what he'd said, I really thought he was going to follow through and do it. As it turns out, this was just the first of many similar occurrences.

At the same time we were putting that deal together, I was still out networking. I didn't just stop when the first or second person I talked to at a business networking event said they were interested. Our goals were big. We wanted to do projects with multiple investors. So I was going to other networking events and meeting other people who were saying exactly the same thing.

"Yeah, I'd invest with you, send me over a deal when you find the next one."

It happened again and again. I'd had at least 10 people say this to me at this point and since the first guy hadn't got back to me, I started sending this deal to other potential investors — all of whom had said they were interested.

Some potential investors did reply when I reached out, but then it turned out they had other criteria or a suitably great excuse for why they couldn't invest. It wasn't necessarily that they didn't want to invest. Often it was just not the right time. Or the deal required more money than they were prepared to invest. Or what has since turned out to be a classic 'Oh sorry, but my funds have JUST been tied up for the next X months'.

Overall we found three categories of reply:

1. **Silence.** Tumbleweed. No reply to an email sent with a deal attached.
2. **'The deal isn't quite good enough.'** Really?! Those numbers were great!
3. **'I've just invested my money in another deal.'** Again, wasted time and energy. Worse — increasing levels of stress!

No matter the reasons, the outcome for us is the same: Two or three weeks of stress and sleepless nights. You don't want to disappoint the vendor or estate agent because those relationships are important. So we keep the 'deal plate' spinning whilst we wait for the 'funding plate' to catch up.

We realised... **you CANNOT build a business this way!**

I started to ponder and reflect on the 'chicken or the egg' problem of **"What comes first, the deal or investor?"** that we were facing here.

When it came to raising finance, it seemed to me there were only three ways of going about it...

1. Find the Deal First.
2. Find the Investor First.
3. Both! Always be raising finance and sourcing deals.

The problem was that each answer had its own set of challenges:

Deal First: "Good deals will always find money!" But, as we were experiencing first hand, this wasn't working in reality!

Investor First: But how on earth do you get an investor to agree to work with you BEFORE you have a deal?! How will they know what they are investing into? Of course they couldn't say 'yes'.

Both Deal and Investor: It just felt totally overwhelming to do it this way, there's WAY too much to do. How on earth are you supposed to do everything, and bring it all together at the same time?

I really felt there must be a better solution than what we were hearing from the rest of the industry.

The Birth of the Investor Pipeline

This frustration of all the wasted time running around trying to raise finance, whilst trying to keep the vendor happy, was the catalyst for us figuring out how to get the money secured from an investor before we had the deal agreed. We realised that to find the right investors and be able to move quickly when we did find deals, we had to start pre-qualifying them and pre-selling our model to them.

The idea of creating an Investor Pipeline was a revelation to us. No one was really talking about it, and if it was being mentioned by people, it certainly wasn't being explained, meaning it ended up being this elusive concept that didn't really work in practice.

And this brings up one of the most important lessons for getting from 'stuck in the nitty-gritty' property investor to 'freedom creating' property investment business owner.

It wasn't enough to have someone say "I'll invest with you. Send me a deal when you find it." We had to build more of a relationship first and make sure potential investors were really interested to invest in what we were doing, and that we felt we could help them to achieve their objectives as well. Part of this was getting potential investors to to agree with our definition of what made a deal 'a deal'. That way we could get all of that agreed BEFORE we had an offer accepted on a deal – it just made it a far more enjoyable experience for everyone involved

This became yet another reason why choosing and focusing on a business model was so important. How else can you get an investor to say 'yes' if they don't actually know what they are investing into? By being specific about our business model, it made it easy to explain it to investors in enough detail that they could buy into it. This simplified the process for getting investors on board, freeing up the time and headspace we needed to continue sourcing at the same time.

Freedom Formula: Develop Your Investor Pipeline Process

Developing your investor pipeline process starts with these six steps:

1. **Get clear on your Business Model.** What does your business actually do? What is the model you are replicating over and over again?
2. **Let go of EVERYTHING that isn't directly related to this.** There's an entire chapter on this later in the book but I wanted to

plant the seed to help you focus. Say it now: I will let go of anything not DIRECTLY RELATED to my chosen business model!

3. **What is your Investor Proposition?** What is the deal criteria that fits underneath your business model? How does that work from a numbers perspective? What is the return on investment? How might you work with other finance to bring the whole deal to life? What's the exit for the money? Until you can answer these questions clearly, you can't create an Investor Proposition. Which means you can't explain to a potential investor what your deals look like, how they work, what the risks and rewards are, or whether the deals fit with what that particular investor is looking for.
4. **Set Clear Expectations with potential investors.** This is an important pre-qualification step. By setting clear expectations, you offer investors who aren't ready — or aren't the right fit — a way out. No hard feelings. No lying awake at night wondering if they get what you propose. No lack of understanding on their part, because you've been crystal clear up front about what you do, how it works, the deal criteria, the returns and the expected time frame to exiting their money.
5. **Qualify Investors who want to work with you on the deals that you want to do.** Now that you have an Investor Proposition, you will have WAY BETTER conversations with investors. It won't be a matter of finding the deal to suit the investor. Instead, you'll say 'this is what we do and if you want to do a deal with us, this is when we expect to do our next deal'. This comes across as more professional to prospective investors and when you do send them the deal (and it is aligned with all the expectations you've already agreed upon), they are much more likely to follow through and invest.
6. **Simplify Your Sourcing of new deals in line with your Business Model.** Once you are clear on your business model, it becomes SO MUCH easier to find deals and actually takes way less time. For example, at one time early in my career, I was known as 'the lady who buys single bed flats in need of refurbishment' in Belvedere & Erith. Estate agents knew what I wanted and called

me first. (I saved more than one chain from falling apart!) They all knew my criteria. Plus, once you get to the point where you are building a team, it is MUCH easier to pass this part of the process to a team member if you have this level of clarity about your business model.

Once you do the above six steps in place, you'll have:

- Qualified Investors lined up who...
- Want to Invest in the Deals you are sourcing.

That's how you find deals and raise finance at the SAME TIME, without disappearing into a sea of overwhelm. Once we developed our process for getting deals funded seamlessly, business was much LESS STRESSFUL.

For more detailed information on how to create your own Investor Pipeline, check the Resources page at the end of the book or visit: www.property-strategy.com/focus

Chapter 4

How Holiday Every Six Weeks Was Born

As my 2015 burnout approached — which I did not see coming at all — my posts on social media got more negative. At that time, I was posting on Facebook roughly five times per week, sharing what we were up to. I'd gone from posting about trying to buy the first property, to every other week posting things like 'Just agreed another one.' Or 'Here's me at a networking event, raising finance'. Or 'I've just been to another investor meeting'. I was posting at crazy times of the night and then again first thing in the morning because I was always out and about at so many events, meetings, oh yes and that little thing called the DAY JOB!

That's when our first business coach contacted me. It was like an angel appeared in the form of Elliot Kay — the partner of a friend I worked with.

Elliot first appeared by sending me a message on social media. I didn't know him well at all. But his message said, 'I'm a bit worried about you. Your posts seem a little bit negative. Do you want to meet for a cup of coffee?'

I knew Elliot was a coach and that he was into personal development. And I was definitely NOT into personal development. That was not my bag. To me it was very woo woo, or 'Hurrah! We're all doing SO WELL. Think POSITIVELY!' I was not on board with all of that. But I wasn't in a great place and appreciated someone caring enough to reach out at a time that I felt fewer and fewer people in my life were 'getting me'. So, I went out and had a coffee with him.

Over coffee, Elliot asked me one of the most important questions I've ever been asked:

"WHY are you doing all this property investing stuff?"

Not only did it help us get back on track, it also became one of the most POWERFUL questions that we've continued to ask ourselves over and over again.

Why the Grind?

At first my answer was something very basic like, "I just want to have enough time to paint my nails." Not very inspiring I know. But I was just SO tired and working SO MANY hours that I'd run out of inspiration and pretty much forgotten why we started in the first place. If I could just have an hour of ME TIME to do my nails, it felt like that would have been a big success at the time!

But that wasn't REALLY why I was doing it. Elliot pushed me to dig deeper and I came out with, "I want to have a nice time with Dave. I want TIME to have a nice time!"

Elliot then said something that helped us start to get clarity:

"You need to know the answer to why you're doing it. If you're not clear *why* you're doing it, maybe you're doing stuff that you don't actually need to do."

That was a wake-up call. When I arrived home, Dave and I started talking about why we were 'doing this property stuff'.

Our answer? We want to go on lots of holidays! It seemed perfectly logical at the time. After all, I'd started the whole journey whilst looking out at the peaceful winter wonderland one morning in France. The problem is, it was still too vague. It was as unclear as our business model. We made our decision that night - we needed this guy to help us get some clarity!

It turns out that Elliot wasn't just a coach, he was specifically a *business* coach. Up until this point, we'd only been working with property trainers and property mentors. We'd never even considered the need for a business coach because, to be honest with you, we didn't think wewere running a business. When we started working with Elliot, we were very quickly disabused of that notion as he introduced us to an incredible new world of business strategy.

One of the first things we presented to Elliot as our new business coach was our 'lots of holidays' motivation. And he came straight back at us asking for more clarity: "So, what is lots of holidays?" Wow, what a question! Dave and I looked at each other blankly... we'd never really thought about being that specific!

Dave and I went back and forth about it, with Dave (as always) really grilling us on the details – he's got a way of asking the most in-depth, revealing questions, that really help us to get clarity. A holiday every four weeks seemed too often and not very practical — we wouldn't get any work done. But every eight weeks seemed too long. In the end we decided that 'lots of holidays' meant every six weeks, which is the moment our new focus was born, creating the #holidayevery6weeks lifestyle! Starting there and then, we looked at everything in our business through the #holidayevery6weeks lens.

How was that going for us? Terribly! We were working seven days a week, every evening, sometimes 18 hours a day. We had no 'spare minutes' left.

Of course, it wasn't just our property business. I was out networking multiple evenings a week. Again, I started to ask WHY? What was I looking for? Based on the advice of others, and the property training I'd had up until that point, I was out there 'building my network'. But I had no clear strategy for what I was really trying to achieve. It turned out that following the generic advice of "focus on building your network" was slowly grinding me down.

Oh, the irony...

Nice Cars, Miserable Lives!

I started looking at the property investors I aspired to be like through a different lens now. When I really looked at them, I realised.... they were always working! They worked evenings and weekends, didn't go on holiday much, and generally looked a bit tired or stressed. Unhealthy. Yes, they drove nice cars but no matter how I looked at it, **I didn't want their life!** I wanted to travel. I did NOT want to be chained to the business as they seemed to be.

That realisation gave me more clarity. To create the life I wanted, I had to be much more CAREFUL about whose advice I was taking. Looking around, it was almost impossible to find people in property who inspired *the life WE wanted.* So we did something that changed our path for the better — forever.

Instead of continuing to learn about more types of property deals and different ways to make money from property, we opted to focus our time on learning about business strategy instead. It seemed much more aligned with creating the life that we wanted. Thankfully, we've never looked back.

Business coaching has been instrumental in helping us shape our business. It provided us with the structure we needed to make sense of how we were setting everything up, and how that would then link to us achieving our end goals. The concepts we were taught are tried and tested in every industry, and businesses of every size have been using them and refining them for hundreds of years. We first worked on this with Elliot. Then he introduced us to his mentor, Deri Llewellyn-Davies. And that is how we first met our great friend and business partner, Dominic Beecheno. Each and every mentor stressed to us the importance of everything stemming from a clear Vision. This really is the starting point of a great business strategy. These business principles are now the real fundamentals of how we work with all of our mentees who are investing in property and it really shifts how you make decisions.

Crafting a Clear Vision

Consider why you first got into property investing. If you are just getting started, think about what made you pick up this book. Most property investors start out with a particular dream in mind. But, in my experience, they often make a big mistake that prevents them from reaching their goals.

For example, I wanted the freedom to go on loads of holidays and the passive income to enable it. When Dave and I first got into property, we did our first deal by reading books. It worked well in the beginning, but after some success we decided it was time to up our game So, we started attending property courses.

We met some really inspirational people who were doing massive things in property. Being around them really stepped up my ambitions and changed my beliefs about what we could achieve. But, as you know, it also created a problem.

These investors didn't just inspire me: I was pulled into THEIR ideas of success because I wasn't clear enough on what success was for me. I thought we needed lots of money, expensive cars and luxury holidays because other property investors had those as their goals. This skewed definition of success led me to saying 'yes' to every type of deal and every opportunity that came my way. Then I started getting pulled into much bigger deals. Yes, they had WAY higher profit margins, but I didn't understand the actual COST of doing it.

The result? Stress. Exhaustion. Putting out fires all the time with FAR too much on my plate. I knew something had to change. We had lost sight of the reason we first got into property: Freedom. Not only financial freedom, but time freedom. We needed to get clearer about what we actually wanted.

We realised that we didn't care about luxury holidays or expensive cars. What we REALLY wanted was to go on simple holidays every six weeks. That clarity gave us a lens to start viewing our business decisions through. From there, we stopped doing things that were moving us away from our dream lifestyle and, instead, within 12-18 months we were taking many more holidays. This brings up one of the most frequently asked questions we get from property entrepreneurs:

"How did you build a property business that you can run from anywhere in the world?"

I'm never surprised when someone asks this question. In my experience, most investors don't get into property solely to achieve financial freedom. They also do it to create lifestyle freedom. The kind of freedom that allows you to run your business — whilst travelling and seeing the world — without being tied to any one place. Which is why Dave and I built a property company that runs, regardless of where we are on the planet.

How to Build a Property Business that Runs Without You

In the autumn of 2020, Dave and I caught up with Elliot. At that meeting he introduced us to one of his friends as 'the guys who have done £7.5 million of property deals between 2014 and 2020'.

On learning this, his friend asked us if Elliot was the reason we owned so much property. To his surprise, after some consideration, we replied, "Actually, NO!"

You see, while Elliot was a brilliant coach who put us on the path to making our dreams a reality, he was actually responsible for us doing FEWER property deals. In fact, if we hadn't worked with Elliot, by that point in 2020 we could well have done £10M-15M of property deals. Instead, we had a £7.5M portfolio.

But here's the thing: while that might have looked EPIC to everyone else, it would have been an absolute mess for us. Because had we done that much property, then we would have been:

- Chained to our desks, with never-ending to-do lists...
- Working every evening and weekend...
- Unhealthy from eating too much junk food, and, more than likely...
- MISERABLE!

Yes, we would have had a bigger property business at that point in time, but it wouldn't have been anywhere near as systemised or able to run without us, and our lives would have been much worse!

That's why working with Elliot was amazing. Because he encouraged us to become focused on what success meant for us. Which in turn laid the foundations for a truly **replicable** and **scalable** business. A business that would allow us to achieve our goal of having the freedom to go on holiday every six weeks much, much sooner!

After translating Elliot's business advice to the property investment world, we were able to focus in on one clear business model, which allowed us to create a simple proposition that attracted the right investors. From there, we just replicated that process over-and-over again. We got better and faster at it. Eventually, we were able to teach it to members of our team who implemented it with minimal involvement from us.

This enabled us to bring more investors on board because they saw how scalable our business was. As a result, we reached a place where we could successfully run — and grow — our property business *from anywhere we wanted to be in the world.* Which is what made me want to get into property in the first place!

Freedom Formula: How to Create Your Dream Life

There are three essential elements to this Freedom Formula:

First, know your 'why'. And I mean really know it. Refine your answer. Our "we want to go on lots of holidays" wasn't specific enough.

Why did YOU start investing in property? Was it to build an epic business that requires you to be chained to your desk? Or do you want a business that runs like clockwork without you and gives you plenty of time and the freedom to travel and enjoy life?

If it's the latter, then my suggestion is that you choose ONE property business model (at least at first) and **get laser focused** on that. Because that will allow you to create a replicable and scalable business that generates plenty of cashflow. And one that doesn't tie you to one location or require you to work 24/7!

Second, make decisions that move you toward YOUR ideal life. Every time you start being drawn in by something that seems 'cool' or 'exciting', ask yourself *is this really my fastest route to achieving my goals? Or am I just being guided by my ego?*

Third, follow those who have created the life you want to create for yourself. This is SO important. Really look at the people who inspire you in property. Are they living the life you want? If not, then take a step back, refocus on your why, and get inspired by someone who has the life you want to create for yourself.

Recipe for Freedom

Sit down now with a notebook and answer these two questions — and be completely honest with yourself:

1. Are you clear on why you first got into property?
2. Do you make every decision in your business with that objective(s) in mind?

This may sound simple, but it isn't easy to do when you're in the thick of it. However, getting crystal clear on what you want and staying true to it is the fastest way I know to:

A. Stop chasing exhausting deal opportunities that aren't a good fit; and
B. Move towards your dream life.

Once you are crystal clear on what you *actually* want (and not what the industry tells you to want) then — and only then — can you build a business that will support your dreams.

Chapter 5

Saying 'Yes' to Every Opportunity COSTS Time, Money, and Freedom

To understand why saying 'yes' can actually SLOW your journey to freedom and COST you time and money, we have to go back to 2015. Every decision I made — from my social life to opportunities and property deals — had consequences.

Interestingly, the word 'decide' stems from the Latin word *decidare* which literally translates "to cut off". To decide is to cut off other possible courses of action. Keep that in mind as you read this chapter.

I QUIT!

By August 2015, I had started to get over my feeling of overwhelm from the first part of the year. While we still hadn't felt the full impact of Shiny Penny Syndrome on our business, I wasn't chasing quite as many. More importantly, I hadn't quit property. As our properties started to get through refurb and get tenanted, they started to bring in money.

Thanks in part to cutting costs using my Finances of Life spreadsheet, I had the confidence to leave my job in market research on the 25th of August 2015.

My final day in market research.

That is me on my final day in market research. My colleagues bought me the hard hat and high-vis vest as a farewell present. I handed in my laptop and company card, they threw me a farewell dinner, and that was it.

Finally... I'd MADE IT!?

All my plans for World Domination were paying off...

Plans For World Domination Notebook. That was my real vibe back then!

That's actually a notebook I had around that time with *Plans For World Domination* on the cover. There was only one problem, a problem you won't hear discussed in the property industry.

Trading One Job for Another

It is one of the greatest myths about escaping the rat race. You read a book or attend a workshop and hear the story about the ideal life...

Sack the boss! Quit the J-O-B!

The problem is, it's not actually true. We've witnessed it — first hand. Yes, you can quit your job thanks to property cashflow... but guess what? You'll have ANOTHER job ready and waiting for you — one that does not grant you ANY annual leave.

That's right, **I actually replaced my job with ANOTHER JOB!** No-one told me about that!

It was full-on. You think you're going to quit your job and suddenly have more time. But there are two big problems and I experienced both.

First, I was so used to working hard that the idea of suddenly leaving my job and not working hard was too much of a shift. I didn't have the blueprint to know how to do it. Even if there hadn't been way too much to do in my new job, it still would have been almost impossible to take it any easier.

After leaving my full-time job, I carried on working nearly as many hours. I'd work from 9:00 a.m. to 7:00 p.m. There was a lot going on in our property business, as at the time we were still trying to do something like seven different business models, and then there were systems and processes to set up so that we could take on a team, and we kept learning and studying to make sure we were clear on what was going on in our business and across the industry.

While it is true that most of my time could now be spent on our property business, it was still long hours. There was not much sign of the freedom I so badly wanted.

Second, I was still getting pulled in too many different directions because of one word...

Yes!

The property industry is like a case study for the Baader-Meinhof phenomenon. Sometimes called *frequency illusion*, it is a cognitive bias where something you recently learned suddenly seems to be everywhere.

When I first started looking into property investing, I was searching for a new and easier way to make money to get me out of my day job, and when I found property investing it was like I suddenly became aware of all these amazing opportunities that were all around me. That thing I had been looking for just kept presenting itself to me again, and again, and again, in so many different formats.

Which is great, right?

The problem is, your mindset is always stuck in the past, in a time when there wasn't much opportunity. It's a dichotomy: There are opportunities everywhere, but your mindset (subconscious mind) is still telling you things are scarce. So what do you do, you start grabbing for every opportunity.

Enter the dreaded FOMO (Fear Of Missing Out). And I had plenty of FOMO...

After our first *Your Property Network* magazine feature, hosts of property networking events started to ask me to speak at their networking events. It all came along rapidly which was exciting.

Of course, I thought I needed to be a public speaker exactly there and then. That was clearly so important it couldn't possibly wait, whilst of course also trying to build a property business. Pretty soon I was travelling around the country speaking at events. I appeared on podcasts. It was a real whirlwind of a time.

In hindsight, it was a TERRIBLE idea! I was doing these talks in different places, trying to be a really great public speaker and win trophies. I even ended up spearheading a brand new 2-day property event specifically for women in property called 'Women Building Wealth' with 3 incredible ladies – Toni Gargan, Rebecca Smith and Catherine Turner.

Yes, it was a great opportunity, with amazing ladies FOR amazing ladies. But was it the opportunity I should have been working on at THAT TIME, whilst also trying to build a property business? NO! It was way too much.

I got completely consumed trying to grab every opportunity. It culminated in opportunity chasing. Pretty soon, we were saying yes to everything; mentorship, speaker training, podcasts... all the time working harder and longer to fit it all in. We didn't quite realise at the time the impact it was having on our business.

Business coaching had helped us gain clarity on what we wanted, but I still had to work out how to do less to achieve more in reality. Constantly looking into exciting new opportunities and learning about different business models had become my standard routine. Then, when impostor syndrome set in, it made me want to go BIG and fuelled even MORE shiny penny syndrome. This nearly culminated in disaster for our property business.

If you want the most direct route to freedom, chasing shiny pennies is NOT advisable! If you ever consider 'doing bigger deals to 10X your property business', remember this story...

The Best Deal We DIDN'T Do

It was 2015, at the height of my Shiny Penny distraction. We wanted to do a commercial to residential conversion, trying to emulate those property investors who were living the life we *didn't* want to live. We were trying to be cool! We convinced ourselves that we loved property because of the wonderful transformations from ugly old properties into beautiful new ones, but looking back it was not LOVE... we just LIKED it. And I promise you *just liking* something is really not a big enough why to get you through the crap that property can throw at you... as we were soon to discover first hand.

As you know, we'd already been looking into doing commercial conversions. We had heard talks, and done courses on doing developments and conversions. We were FIRED UP and READY TO GO BIG!

We'd analysed loads of different opportunities. We'd looked into part burnt down buildings and tried to source developments. Then we found THE commercial conversion. FINALLY! A deal that would work — the best deal we'd come across — and it was very exciting! It all stacked up and looked like it made sense.

The existing building had two floors we could convert into 12 or 13 standard flats — the numbers just about worked based on that. Even better, the building next door was higher, and our planning consultant was confident we could get planning permission for another floor. The third floor would give us another seven or eight flats making the deal a no brainer.

It was like all the work, all the preparation, everything we'd learned attending training events was coming together in ONE deal. We finally knew what questions to ask a planning consultant. We had a builder; Dave took him around to the property and it felt good. Dave's only reservation was that all we'd done so far was single let 1-bed flats and one HMO, so were we really ready for this?

Me? I just KNEW we were ready to stop 'wasting' our time on the little refurb projects we'd done up until that point and to do something PROPER with our property investing time. We were ready to make our MILLIONS in the shortest possible timeframe! We'd heard others in the industry stand on stages and say, "Commercial conversions are just refurbs with another couple of zeros on the end. That's it. Don't worry about it!"

So I said, "Dave, don't you worry about that. Add the zeros. It's not £10,000, it's £100,000 or £1 million. Just get over it, Dave. *Change your mindset.* Don't worry about it, Dave!"

The numbers were phenomenal. We estimated the total project cost at £2,018,861. The gross development value (GDV) was projected at £2,815,000 for a profit of nearly £800,000. We just KNEW we were going to be rich!

Thankfully, our business mentor started asking us some tough questions.

Saved! (By Our Business Mentor)

We excitedly showed this deal to our business mentor Deri and he put a RIGHT DOWNER on it!! The conversation went something like this...

DERI

Do you have the power team to be able to deliver on this kind of project?

US

We are looking for them right now.

DERI

Do you know what power team you actually need to be able to deliver on these projects? And who actually does what?

US

Yes, we are confident we do.

DERI

Are you sure — 100% — on your development figures?

US

We've done our deal analysis and have had training from experts who do this all the time!

DERI

Do you understand what you are RISKING here?

US

There's so much profit in it that even if things go wrong, we should be OK!

DERI

You've got a great small refurb / portfolio business that is working. Something that you can sensibly scale with minimal risk. Why are you trying to do something else?

US

BECAUSE THERE'S SO MUCH MONEY TO BE MADE!

No one else in the property world was giving us this REALITY CHECK. From what we'd heard, moving into developments seemed straightforward and we'd got drawn into it. But Deri was really negative about it.

Most importantly, Deri had previously had negative experiences of investing property. He wasn't just looking at the numbers, he had experience and knowledge of everything that could go wrong. And because of this he was the first one who'd been negative. He said something like, 'I really don't think you guys should be doing it. You do what you want, but you don't have my blessing for this project.'

Deri kicked our a—! He was the first person to really call us out on our crap. His approach was more balanced — it wasn't "Go BIG or go home and grab EVERY opportunity!" He let us know that we could destroy ourselves financially with one project if it didn't work out.

We didn't abandon the project straight away but it made us question everything. We went from thinking we can do this... to looking deeper and putting more care and attention into every aspect of the project. Ultimately, we realised Deri was right, we didn't know enough about anything. So, after careful reflection about the risk involved, and a lot more questions of our power team, we decided we were way out of our depth and walked away.

Commercial Conversions: Cool Until They're Not

This all happened almost nine years ago. Looking back, the answers we gave Deri were SO WRONG, and I am soooo glad we didn't do that deal!

The truth is:

- We didn't have the power team in place. We didn't even really know who we actually needed!
- Our deal analyser (whilst looking comprehensive) had SO many holes in it!
- We were putting our entire portfolio at risk. Everything we'd done up to then was on the line for this ONE project!
- And... We were trying to do something new, something bigger because it seemed more exciting. It was just another shiny penny!

Looking back on it now, it was the best deal we DIDN'T do. We were being impatient. We nearly jumped into the deep end to prove ourselves, and we could have destroyed ourselves and everything we'd built so far trying to do it.

Think about it. If you were a lawyer: would you expect to be able to take on a billion pound civil case without a law degree and in-court experience on smaller cases? NO! If you were a pilot: would you expect to be able to fly a jumbo jet without first learning how to fly a small plane, then a medium sized plane, and then a large plane? NO!

The moral of the story: Patience.

This is me paying it forward and giving YOU a (loving) butt kicking — passing on the 'be careful' warning that we were so lucky to have received.

If you are considering moving into conversions or developments and you haven't built up the proper experience and team along the way (doing gradually larger projects), then please think carefully before you plunge in. The fact is you don't know what you don't know!

Remember, small deals done in a systemised way can get you the same results in the long run, but with much less risk. The property business is a marathon, not a sprint.

Chapter 6

Do Less to Do More

In property, there's a time lag between you doing something and seeing the outcome. It takes a good three to six months to buy a property and another three to six months to refurbish it and rent it out. So it's easily a good twelve months before you see results (let alone income) from your hard work and labour. This is particularly true if you try to do multiple business models at the same time or chase shiny pennies. You feel really busy putting in offers and taking action, but you don't realise you're getting distracted.

Because we'd been through a really focused phase in the beginning doing single lets, we still had deals coming through and completing. The time lag meant that the work we'd done 6-12 months prior was paying off, and it felt as if the payoff was coming from up in the work we were doing at the time. What we didn't realise, was that the work we were doing at the time wasn't working, and what was working was all stemming from a past phase when we had been very focused.

As you know, at the end of 2014 and into early 2015, we had agreed quite a lot of single let deals in a short space of time. As those properties went through the purchase progression and then through refurb, the Shiny Penny was creeping in. We started trying to do loads of other stuff, or as the industry likes to put it, we started to 'diversify to lower our risk'. Soon we would see the results of all that diversification...

However, none of that mattered. We KNEW all our hard work was going to pay off. It would all be worth it because in the end, it would be AMAZING! So we kept pushing, viewing dozens, if not hundreds, of properties... scheming, analysing, and planning world domination. The outcome of all of our hard work in 2015-16?

In 2016, we did... drum roll please...

One deal. ONE DEAL! One single flat. ONE! That's it. It was SO FRUSTRATING because we were working harder than ever. There I was, having started in the property world because I was looking for an opportunity to change my life, to have more choice, more time, and more freedom. Instead, I was killing my own dream by saying 'yes' to everything. The good news is, there IS a BETTER WAY!

Just Say 'NO' to Success

This was a painful lesson to learn, but ultimately our pain and failure ended up being a lesson we can gift to others. So here it is...

You don't need to try and monetise every opportunity and every deal that crosses your desk.

You will feel productive, but it will be a LOT of wasted time and energy. By trying to do everything, ultimately you will trap yourself in a limited cash flow cycle. Why? Because you can't put any replicable process around something that is different every single time. You'll also take longer to analyse deals, and that lack of speed will mean you miss the RIGHT opportunities for you.

If you are currently doing something simple like single let flats, and you're thinking to yourself *I'm growing a bit slowly, wouldn't it be nice and easy to just do some blocks of flats as well?* Then I'm here to tell you from hard earned experience... it wouldn't! In fact, these two seemingly similar models are very different. They have different sourcing methods, different deal criteria, different things to check on viewings, different analysis methods, different mortgage products, different valuation methodologies, different levels of finance required, different returns, the list goes on and on. You get my drift! In fact, the only similarity between these two models is the word 'flats' and the fact that you are renting to the same type tenants (e.g. students, professionals, etc.).

Similarly, if you are more experienced and are doing a more complex model like commercial conversions to HMOs, and you're thinking to yourself, *why not just do a few commercial conversions to blocks of flats at the same time, it's basically the same thing?* Well sorry to say, no they aren't.

You may well have enough build experience to be able to safely transition to blocks of flats without too much business risk, but in terms of systems and processes, you have just set back your ability to become replicable and scalable by about 12 months! And you've just chained yourself to the business for that amount of time as well!

Who's going to make all the decisions around how many flats can fit in and what size they need to be? Who's going to do the detailed analysis to work out whether it stacks with 3 x 2 bed flats, or whether it needs to be 5 x 1 beds and 1 x 3 bed? Who's going to decide what the refurb specification needs to be now that the tenant type and valuation method has changed? Who's going to find out what the banks are happy with or aren't happy with when it comes to blocks of flats? Who's going to work out how the fire regulations differ for a block of flats vs an HMO? That's right, all of that and much more will fall on your shoulders, filling up your already overwhelming to-do list with even more jobs. This is just another set of hurdles to overcome before everything can become replicable and able to be delegated.

You may be thinking 'I'll just get my power team to do all the above'... well wait until you've read our experience of doing our first commercial conversion in 2017 before you choose that route, because that's exactly what we thought!

Remember, if you can't make it replicable, then it's NOT a business! It's a job. (Which is fine if you want a job of course... but not if you don't!)

If it's not replicable, it will always be reliant on you. If that's the case, then it is limited by how many hours you have in a day and you'll never be able to get too far away from your business. It will always need you.

There is a COST to monetising every opportunity and trying to make every deal you come across work. You won't see the difference in the short term. You might actually feel BETTER, because you'll feel busy and productive!! It will even feel like you're problem solving and overcoming challenges by finding creative ways to make anything work... which is a good thing right?

But give it a few months or years...

You will see a dramatic difference between A) those who were able to focus, commit and say 'no' and B) those who said 'yes' to every opportunity.

Group A is probably in some far-flung corner of the world living their best life. Group B? Well, they are most likely overworked, exhausted, staring into their laptop late into the night, surrounded by paperwork and a to-do list that just won't quit.

So, that deal you 'need to analyse'? Ask yourself: Do you really need to analyse it? Or is it time to say 'no'?

Freedom Formula: Trying to Monetise Every Opportunity Is COSTING You!

Now you know. Whether you're a seasoned property investor or just getting started, this one mindset shift can change your life for the better.

When the next amazing opportunity presents itself (and it will), or you sit down to find some creative solution to make a deal work, first ask yourself...

Is this really the right opportunity for me? Or is it time to say 'no'?

Then imagine your life in five years if you instead focused on creating a truly replicable business model and investor proposition that can propel you towards freedom. Do you really want to monetise every opportunity that comes across your desk? Or do you want to build a property business that can give you freedom to travel and spend quality time with your family?

If it's the latter, then you need to do more deals — and plenty of them. So to make this happen, you'll need three things...

1. A laser-focused sourcing process that leads to quick offers and great deals.
2. Consistent and reliable financing, i.e., the money, lined up and ready to go, so you can keep snapping up great deals as you secure them. And...
3. To ensure the amount of time YOU put in to make it all happen is decreasing with every new deal. For that, you need to create a business where systemising and hiring is SIMPLE.

With these things in place, you will be ready to ramp up the number of deals you can do and, ultimately, the amount of cashflow you can create. Better yet, you won't even be bothered that loads of potential opportunities are passing you by, because you'll be creating cash and freedom for yourself.

And wasn't that the point of all this in the first place?

Time to Refocus: How to Look Beyond the Shiny Penny

It had been a tough time, trying to do too many different things:

- Too many types of property deals, because we'd heard "diversify to reduce risk" and we thought *THIS looks COOL!*
- Becoming a property trainer
- & public speaker
- 1-2-1 mentoring to other property investors

It was too much. At the same time, we realised we were spinning too many plates and needed to focus, the property market was going up. At first we were buying single lets in our area for under £110k, but now we were buying them for £130k-£140k.

To complicate matters, prices continued to go up and the whole mechanics of the deal shifted. For example, by the time we got to refinance, values were more like £200k, but the rents weren't going up in line with values which meant yields were going down. Eventually the banks increased their stress tests and we were no longer able to release enough money on refinance to make it worthwhile.

Our model was breaking itself. I had wanted to invest in an area with strong capital appreciation as that seemed like a wise investment choice. What I didn't realise was that by doing this it would reduce the amount of time our model would work there. And because we didn't have enough clarity about what model we were doing, it ended up taking quite a few months before we realised what the problem was. Once we recognised the problem, we found our focus again by moving to a new area.

Thanet Ticked Every Box

At this point I'd left my job, Dave had left his job, and we were totally location free. We decided to open our minds and consider the whole of the UK in our search for a new investment area. However, it didn't take Dave long to realise that it would take forever if we had too many variables to analyse... With his incredible analytical mind he got us to chose a list of five specific criteria that we were looking for in an investment location and we got analysing. This allowed us to do a really quick analysis of loads of different parts of the UK, including Bristol, Edinburgh, Manchester, Cardiff... in fact anywhere that struck our fancy.

The five key variables we focused on were:

Bedrooms: We knew that re-configuring the layout to add bedrooms was a great way to add value to a property. But we needed to make sure that by adding a bedroom it definitely added enough value compared with the cost of works required.

Our metric was simple: How much difference was there in value between a one bed and a two bed in each area? We knew that adding a bedroom would cost, say, £3,000 to build a wall and redecorate. And If we needed to move a kitchen it would be a bit more. Based on experience, we knew we needed to see at least a 25% uplift in value from the one bed to two bed properties to make this method work. We did the same for two beds to three beds, knowing that if adding a bedroom raised the value by 25%, the numbers would make sense.

Capital Appreciation: We wanted to invest in an area with good capital appreciation and growth. So we did a capital appreciation analysis of the previous 20 years. We wanted to see at least a certain amount of growth over each 10-year period to suggest that the area had potential to continue growing strongly.

Yields: If yields were too low, our model wouldn't work. So we looked at the average gross yield for each area. And we did it by a simple method: Looking at Rightmove. We would just look at one bed properties in each area, and then go to the very middle page and find the middle (median) property. The price of that property gives you an easy read on average prices in the area. Then we did exactly the same for rent. We then used this to figure out the average gross rental yield for each area. For our model, we wanted this to be over 7%.

Stock: We wanted there to be enough stock of the type of properties we were looking for. It wouldn't make sense to move to an area without enough properties that fit our criteria.

Commercial Opportunities: I was still holding on to the idea of 'moving up' to commercial conversions. Even though I knew I'd chased one too many shiny pennies already, and we really didn't have experience with commercial conversions, it was still one of our five variables for choosing a new area. I had just resigned myself to 'starting smaller' with say a 4-unit conversion, rather than an 18-unit one.

In the end, using this method made choosing a new area really straightforward. We just filtered areas out. Most places only had two of those metrics covered. Some had three. But only ONE place we looked at had all five — Perfect!

Even better, this whole analysis process only took one afternoon. Rid of any doubt, we decided that Thanet would be our new investment location... and we would be moving to Margate to make it all happen!

Focus and Rhythm

It was the end of 2016, going into 2017, when we found our focus again. Our thinking was that buying blocks of flats was the way to scale up. Instead of just buying one flat, you buy four. It turns out that it actually wasn't that easy[1]. Still, we did find our focus again with blocks of flats. Now, at that time our idea of what counted as a block of flats was really quite broad. But that's where we decided to focus and it was good enough to get us going again.

Over the next few months, this renewed focus paid off, and we agreed three blocks of flats. The first ever block of flats we bought consisted of four flats on one freehold. We also bought a block of six flats on the seafront. And the third property was our first commercial conversion, a mid-terrace consisting of one shop and two flats to be converted into a block of four flats. (Yes, I convinced Dave eventually! But only once he'd massively upgraded our deal analyser!)

We agreed all three deals within 3-6 months of this decision. The block of four flats and the commercial conversion we'd agreed within a month of moving to Margate. The block of six flats was agreed in early 2017. It was like *Boom! We've nailed it! Time to scale!*

1. More on why that wasn't true in Chapter 9: Lessons from the Worst Deal We Ever DID

Chapter 7

Take a Systemised Approach Instead of Systemising

It was late 2016/early 2017 and we had started to find our focus again and the deals were flowing! It was such a relief, we'd cracked the nut (again!). So it made me start to reflect on where I'd gone wrong over the last 18 months.

Why ANOTHER Property Training Course Was Not the Answer

I realised we'd been so overwhelmed and so unclear on why we were working so hard (for so little results), that we were desperate for any solution. At the time, it seemed like the solution was always... "another property strategy". We must be working on the wrong thing, there must be a better strategy, and so therefore we must need another course to learn the magical new property strategy so we can implement as quickly as possible. We had done courses on buy-to-let, commercial conversions, developments, and public speaker training. I even signed up to some sort of network marketing course at one point!

With the benefit of hindsight I started to realise I had done... TOO. MUCH. TRAINING!! It wasn't focused enough. WE weren't focused enough. We were spending more money — and more time — unnecessarily. We didn't need to do more courses and learn more strategies.

By not being focused, it meant I was just trying to do more things to solve the problem. Not only were we NOT solving the actual problem, but we were also making it WORSE! A lot worse!

Business Strategy

Our first business coach, Elliot Kay, helped us come to the realisation that we weren't 'just investing in property', we were 'building a business'. Part of the reason we were so overwhelmed was that we just hadn't realised this. (Looking back I can't quite believe how I couldn't see the wood for the trees!) If you've got a business, you need a business plan, right? I'd heard of a business plan, but I had no idea how to make one! So under Elliot's guidance, we started learning how to work with an amazing tool called *Strategy on a Page*.

BGI Strategy on a Page™

With the property training I'd done up until that point, I'd always gone solo. I'd go and 'get the knowledge', sift through it, and report back to Dave with what he would actually find interesting and useful. But now that we were working on business strategy, we decided Dave had to be involved as we were now making big future plans that impacted us both. It was a very important shift in the dynamic of our working relationship and business focus – particularly as we both saw the world through such different perspectives. It was becoming clear that I was more genius when it came to the big picture planning, whereas Dave was better at making sense when there of things when it got very granular and detailed when it came to finding a way through. Both perspectives coming together made for some, shall we say, very healthy 'debates' sometimes!

It was get to have a moderator to find the middle ground between us. It was great to have someone asking us "What do you guys want? Why are you building this business?" which was an odd question at the time. Up to that point, I didn't think I was building a business, I was just investing in property.

We figured out our vision, purpose, and values — the north star for where we were heading over the next 5-10 years, why we were doing it, and what types of people we wanted to work with. We worked on our market positioning and our short, mid and long term strategy. Then there were the key numbers behind our growth — our business growth indicators (BGIs).

So we completed the whole 1-pager (it probably took about 20 hours in total) with Elliot the first time round. It was brilliant. It was exactly what we needed to start thinking of it as a business. The only caveat was that even though Elliot was a business coach, his expertise was in speaker training. He wasn't a property guy. He helped us make this plan, but with no real knowledge of property. So once we'd finished working with Elliot, he suggested we work with his mentor, Deri, who DID have experience of property.

Property Strategy

Elliot linked us up with Deri Llewellyn-Davies, the guy who actually created *Strategy on a Page*. Funnily enough, that is also how I ended up on a call with Dominic Beecheno — now our Property Strategy business partner, fellow mentor to our clients and the writer of the foreword on this book! On that call, Dom talked with me about attending one of Deri's 3-day business retreats.

It seemed like a no brainer because Deri was the guy who created this awesome tool we were using, and he had some experience in property. Six months after completing our first ever business strategy, we found ourselves sitting around a table with a group of inspired business owners across a variety of industries, working to take our business to a new level.

It was whilst we were on that retreat that we had a MASSIVE revelation that continues to impact how we operate and what we teach. We realised that every single business model that we were doing (or trying to do!) actually needed its very own *Strategy on a Page*. HMOs, commercial conversions, title splits, developments, speaking... Each was actually a DIFFERENT page, with its own DIFFERENT strategy! Yikes!

So within the first 24 hours of working with Deri, we went from feeling super confident with our one business plan — on one page — to having to create SEVEN new business plans! All different from each other. It was mind-boggling to say the least!

There we were on a 3-day retreat where the intent was to refine your business plan, and we suddenly had seven different plans to work on. And you know, we were very tenacious. Against Deri's sage advice to focus on a couple, we instead tried our absolute best to fill them all out. Now I'm telling you, even doing one of those properly in three days is enough. But seven? It was just overwhelming. We came away from that retreat with seven half completed business plans that weren't really that useful to us.

So the silver lining of going on this retreat was clarity. We were building a business and we needed a business plan. But all these different models — which we thought were different flavours of diversification — were actually different businesses. We thought we were building one business, when actually we were struggling with seven. NO WONDER I was getting burnt out!!

It still took us a few months after the retreat to finally come to the realisation that with so many different business models it was chaos — we were always going to be working a LOT of hours. And we were very clear that was NOT the plan. So gradually we started to let go of trying to do everything, and started to focus in on the parts that would get us to our goals quickest.

Blocks of flats had started to work really well, and we were STILL shiny eyed about commercial conversions — so when it came to property, we made the decision to go all in on these two things.

Paying It Forward

When Dave and I were doing loads of property training and mentorship, it was great because it got us to take massive action. However, it also took us down SO MANY cul de sacs. Then when we started investing into business mentorships, they helped us to create structure in our business. This was a revelation for us, but it highlighted an issue: Property mentors weren't teaching about business strategy and business mentors weren't teaching how to apply it to property investing.

The more I put into business strategy, the more passionate I was about it. When I shared my passion and excitement with Deri he said, "Why don't I train you to be able to use this for other people?"

So I went and did some training with Deri about what the 'behind the scenes' of the page was. I learned what it meant to deliver it as a business coach. Off the back of that, I then took *Strategy on a Page* out into the property world, working with other property investors to go through the same process we'd been through with Elliot and Deri. However, there was one big difference: My unique blend of skills and experience.

I brought together a passion for business strategy with hands-on experience of building a property investment business from the ground up. It was a brilliant combination of skills, and something I felt the property investment industry was desperately in need of. Yes, I could make a lot more money doing property deals, but what I was doing as part of my business, Property Strategy, felt like much more of a deep calling and something I HAD to do.

The Downside of Strategy

Eventually, we found that the magic piece is somewhere between the two — bringing together property training and business training. That's why we started Property Strategy in the first place. We realised the property industry needs to know this — to bring these two things together. Property knowledge and expertise AND business strategy and growth principles — so you can invest in property WITHOUT creating another job for yourself.

Business strategy was brilliant and it got us looking at how we were doing things in a totally different light. There was way more structure. There was way more clarity about things that we hadn't realised before. It helped us to start moving the business forward in a very different direction with much more clarity about OUR vision and how WE could make that a reality.

However, we subsequently realised there was a bit of a downside. Business strategy had so many different threads to it, and we tried to focus on them all equally. So it was no longer just about finding deals and investors, we suddenly had all these other aspects to consider:

- What systems are needed to be able to deliver on everything?
- What processes will you need and how are you building them?
- What financial management reports are needed and who's providing them?
- What will you need in your cashflow forecast?
- What about your monthly management accounts?
- How are you tracking your KPIs?
- What KPIs are you tracking?
- How and when do you review data to make better decisions?
- How are you building your team?
- When are you hiring team members?
- How are you helping team members to grow and develop?

Suddenly there was all this other stuff that we had to do and it split our focus. Deals, investors, operations, finance, team... we ended up giving equal weighting to all those different areas. I subsequently realised that was a mistake because **there are different aspects of strategy that are important at different phases.**

At first when I started working with people creating their strategies, I was quite anal about making sure they had a whole beautiful plan. I wanted to see a completely filled-out one page, all lovely, neat, and tidy. And I wanted to know that they focused on all of it. But actually I realised that's not what's most important.

There are a few key elements that are important depending on what phase you're at. If you're just trying to get off the ground, you've got to be clear and focused about what deals you're doing, and how it's working with investors. You have to focus on moving THOSE parts of the business forward. Because if you don't get that working, you haven't got a business.

If you have already got deals and investors working, you don't want to keep pushing and working on those. Instead, you want to get team members coming in to help. Which means you need to be clear on the necessary processes. So you have to know WHAT part of the business strategy to push at different phases, and what to deprioritise. It became really clear that we hadn't learnt this along the away.

What is the priority? And When?

By focusing in this way, you can have a great plan and move in the direction of your vision. It will help you to keep your foot on the gas, taking you in the direction of doing more deals and raising finance, but with a more structured and systemised approach. This was the big lesson that we've taken forward into our methodology in Property Strategy: making decisions based on a great business strategy AND a deep knowledge of the property investment industry, so that you know what order to do things in to get the best, quickest results when it comes to doing more deals.

Evolution: The Property Strategy Business Plan

Ultimately, we ended up evolving. Inspired by *BGI's Strategy on a Page* (and with Deri's blessing) we created the *Property Strategy Business Plan*[1]. We adjusted the emphasis around some of the language, changing it to be more relevant to property.

There are key differences between *Strategy on a Page* and the *Property Strategy Business Plan.*

Strategy on a Page has five key areas of strategy including marketing, sales, operations, finances, and people. Those are universal to almost all businesses. What we found in property is that these didn't quite make sense so we adjusted them accordingly.

1. See the Resources page at the end of the book to download the *Property Strategy Business Plan*

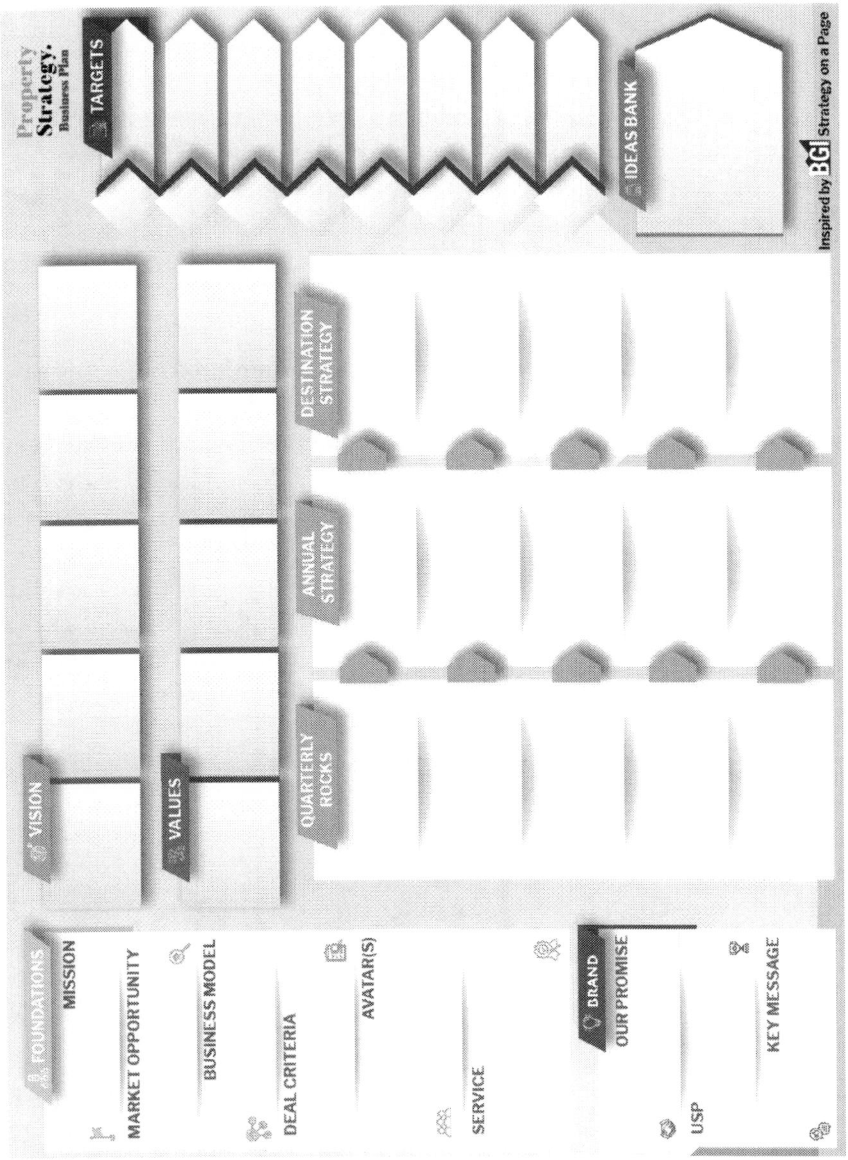

Property Strategy Business Plan

In the *Property Strategy Business Plan,* the key areas of your strategy are:

- Sourcing and Acquisition (Deals)
- Funding (Investors)
- Delivery
- Financial Management
- Team

One big shift was realising there are actually two marketing strategies and two sales pipelines. There's a marketing strategy to find deals and a marketing strategy to find investors. Then there's a sales pipeline for securing deals and a sales pipeline for securing investors. It's this combination of marketing and sales and how these two pipelines need to come together simultaneously that makes property companies more complex compared to many other businesses.

Marketing, Sales, Deals, Investors

For a while we tried to shoehorn deals and investors into the marketing area, and deals and investors into the sales area. We subsequently realised it was not a helpful way to think about it. It needed to be flipped around. So as we went through the iterative process to create the *Property Strategy Business Plan,* this was one of the big changes. Instead of Marketing and Sales, it became Deals and Funding. Those were the two different departments. So Deals encompasses marketing and sales for finding deals, and Funding encompasses marketing and sales for finding investors.

When we started to think about it like this, it was a real game-changer. We realised that this was one of the reasons that having a clear business model was so important.

With a clear business model, it is easier to define what a deal actually is to you. And with that clarity, it's so much easier to communicate to the people you work with to help you to find deals. Whether you're doing direct to vendor, working with agents,or working with sourcers, knowing exactly what a deal looks like and what the numbers need to be, are important parts of being able to communicate it. Then, when an opportunity comes along through the marketing, it is very clear whether you should say yes or no. It either fits or it does not. Sometimes opportunities that come through aren't deals yet - maybe they need some serious negotiation, or maybe it's just a matter of time passing while the sellers motivations change. But it's your clarity about what you're actually looking for, and having a pipeline that you continue to follow up on over time, that makes the deals happen.

So clarity around your business model informs your criteria for deals and how you find them. It also informs what sort of investors are right for your deals and how you communicate that to them.

You need to know what dealsyou're doing, how that actually works, and what the numbers are. Then by having that clarity, you can communicate with potential investors and ensure you find people who are actually aligned with what you do and how you can help them.

Like with deals, potential investors may come to you, but if they are not interested in the sorts of deals you are doing, you want to be able to say, "No, I'm not the right person for you to work with" sooner rather than later. For those who are right, taking them through a really nice pipeline process ensures you comply with FCA regulations AND that you're the right fit to work together. This is how you get investment lined up before you've got a deal agreed so you don't have any sleepless nights.

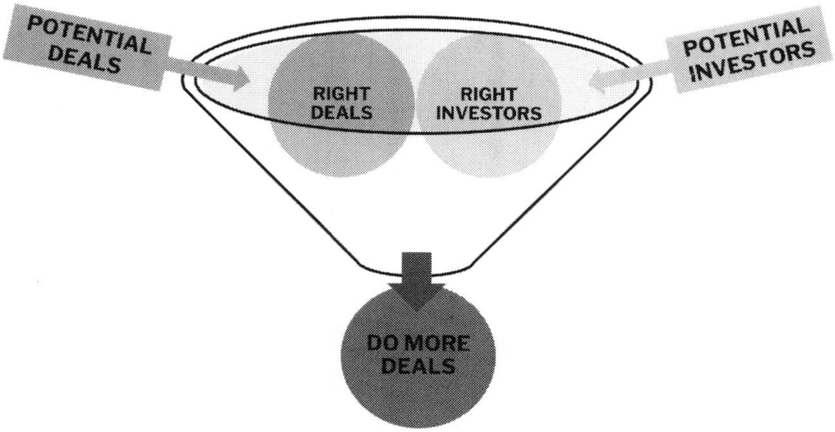

Marketing & Sales for Property Investors

Ultimately, this entire evolutionary process helped us learn to specialise.

Choosing Courses and Mentors with Focus

Prior to applying business strategy, we were grabbing onto any property training that came along for dear life, hoping it was the magic bullet solution, which of course doesn't exist! Learning about business strategy helped us to think about our business in a more structured way. This, in turn, allowed us to identify problems that would have been hard (or even impossible) to identify otherwise.

For example, at this point we were tracking KPIs and asking questions to get to the root of any problems. *Is this a marketing problem? Is it a sales problem? Is it a systems problem?* In this way we were able to pinpoint problems and then, off the back of that, identify what kind of support we needed. We could then go and find the right training or mentor to fill that gap. This was a far cry from waiting to be sold to by someone claiming to have the magic bullet.

This helped us to gain even more clarity about what we needed to move our business forward. It gave us the confidence to say 'yes' to the support we did need, and 'no' to anything that wasn't right for us.

Deep, Not Wide

Learning to go deep on your business model will speed up your progress. The sooner you figure this out, the faster you can scale. Specialism and gaining expertise (focus) is like putting your foot on the accelerator.

In contrast, saying 'yes' to everything (lack of focus) is like putting your foot on the accelerator AND the brakes — it wastes a lot of energy, creates friction and will slow you down because there's far more to learn.

Most people invest in property in a way where it just becomes another job for them. That 'passive income' you've heard so much about? It IS possible, but you have to start treating it like a business. Be careful who you follow. Pick a business model, specialise and become the expert in that model, and stick with it.

Who's Driving?

Before we came up with our holiday every six weeks idea, we'd looked at what others were doing and thought *I should really listen to you because you seem experienced.* However, with our new vision, our perspective shifted. We began looking at others and wondering *is that person living the life that I want?* I realised that if someone isn't living the life I want, then I shouldn't be taking their advice on how to build my business.

That's why our #holidayevery6weeks concept was so pivotal in our business growth. It provided the impetus, clarity, and focus required to help us shift away and find a new path forwards. We were able to say to ourselves "Right, that community is great for energy and inspiration but let's choose our own direction."

So the advice I would give to anyone now wanting to achieve more Freedom from their business starts with asking this question:

Are you driving your property business, or is it driving you?

When we are passionate about our business, it's easy to lose ourselves in it — working all hours under the sun, without rest, to make sure everything is on the right track. This might work for a while, but as your business grows, doing everything yourself starts to become impossible. If you force yourself to do it, you will become overwhelmed. Eventually, it leads to burnout.

My 2015 burnout experience made me realise that nothing good comes out of constantly working IN the business. Managing team members, handling customer service issues and administrative tasks — all are important. But they distract you from focusing on the bigger picture and taking your property business to the next level.

To be successful, you need to work ON the business. This means that YOU, as the business owner, need to find the time to focus on strategic planning, growth, and development. You need to regularly take a step back from the daily grind so that you can look at the big picture and know where to focus. This is when you can develop long-term strategies, analyse market trends, seek out new opportunities, and make decisions that will drive growth and success.

As you work on the business, it will seem as if you need to 'systemise' it. That means choosing to do things in a replicable way and identifying operational tasks that you can delegate to team members. However, this is where you have to be careful, because you can easily lose sight of your vision...

Take a Systemised Approach, Rather Than 'Systemising'

Having a clear business plan really helped us to stay focused and committed to a systemised approach. We could see which areas of the business needed work, what we needed to do, and when to do it. We could see how what we did this week, this month, and this year ultimately linked into our vision.

When it comes to growing a property business, one of my big revelations has been to take a systemised approach rather than 'systemising'. When you've got a clear business model, and you're focused on growing in a strategic way, every deal you do is similar. You replicate it over and over again. And because you're replicating it over and over again, it gets simpler every time. You fill in the knowledge gaps, learn the lessons, and refine how you do things. This is the balance between the chaos of having no systems and the complete order of everything being 'systemised'.

By being focused, doing less, and systemising the actions that you take, you create a replicable *process*. However, that doesn't mean you have to necessarily sit down and write them up.

When we first decided to 'systemise', I got sucked into the perfection trap. I was spending DAYS writing up process documents and standard operating procedures. This is what I learnt from doing it the wrong way: I spent too much time trying to organise things. In a growing business there is not enough time as it is, never mind with you trying to sit down and 'systemise' and write things up. Every day I did THAT was a day I wasn't out there hustling for deals or meeting new investors. I wasn't doing the income generating tasks.

If you do things the same way every time and don't deviate, then you start to naturally create a process for how your business runs (without having to allocate entire days to this task). Once your cashflow has built up, you'll have the financial resources to hire someone. Then, when it is time to bring in someone to help, it is much easier to work out which parts to delegate first. And it will be easier to brief them on your processes because you've taken a replicable approach to building the business. Then you can ask THEM to write that up for you, rather than you spending time to do it.

This approach takes a load of stuff off your to-do list, it prevents you going too far into chaos, and keeps you at that nice borderline between order and chaos where the REAL progress happens and cashflow really grows. That was the biggest takeaway that we had in terms of bringing together business strategy and property investment in a way that gets the best, fastest, quickest results.

Recipe for Freedom:
How to Train Your First Team Members the Easy Way

To start, you'll need to download screen recording software such as Camtasia, Loom, Zappy, Screenpal, or Quicktime.

- Using the screen recording software, do your normal process from start to finish, but talk through what you are doing as you do it.
- Save the recording onto a cloud-based software for use as the primary training on how to do that job.
- When your team member first watches the video, ask them to create and save a simple 'process document' to use as a 'cheat sheet' for future reference. This doesn't need to be complex. And once your team member has done the process the first time by following the video, this process document serves as their reminder of the steps next time.

Chapter 8

Nailed It!

Our journey to freedom started out like a roller coaster; we experienced the highest of highs and the lowest of lows. I battled through Shiny Penny Syndrome, Impostor Syndrome, and burnout. I chased every property opportunity under the sun because I thought that what everyone else was doing was better than what we were doing. Sometimes we chose the wrong investment partners or listened to people in the industry who weren't being transparent and weren't living the life we wanted to live. We spent precious time analysing deals that led to nothing.

So. Much. Wasted. Time!

The purpose of this book is to help you avoid making the same mistakes we made so that YOU can get to freedom faster.

Looking back, we've come a long way, but it hasn't always been easy. Rather than sugar coating it, you need to know the truth. Full transparency: Some of what we did was very painful.

Pain and Progress

There have been tears. There have been arguments. There have been struggles getting to sleep and mornings waking up early, WORRYING about some element of the business. Dave and I have experienced burnout multiple times. Building a property business is DEFINITELY not for everyone. I used to think anyone could do it, but I'd actually recommend most people NOT do it!! It is not for the faint hearted.

I'm really not selling it, am I?!

But THIS IS THE REALITY.

I make the effort to reflect on this every year around my birthday to keep me grounded in how far we've come. Because even though we are now in a constant stream of adventure whilst running our property business remotely, I'll never take it for granted.

Has it been worth it?

For me, a thousand times yes. We've created the right life for us. A life of freedom and choice.

Lest you start to wonder if this whole property dream is worth it for you, let's look at what happened as we started to figure things out.

It wasn't all grind the whole time. We had phases of getting focused, then getting distracted. We went from no focus, to focus, and then we would chase another Shiny Penny. Eventually, we realised that when we had focused on 1-bed, buy-to-let flats, we scaled fast. Really fast. When we tried to diversify, we stalled; nothing happened.

If we had carried on trying to do lots of different models, we would have carried on stalling. As soon as we chose blocks of flats and focused on it, we scaled really fast again. That's how we managed to get four of them (25 flats in total) in under year, more than doubling the size of our portfolio. Now that's what I call scaling!

It's not to say that every property and every project we do is easy or without problems. That's not really how it works. And it hasn't been linear. We've stepped back from elements of the business only to jump back in when we were let down. And we've been let down by SO MANY people in the industry. For example, site managing a project that was getting off track in the Autumn of 2017 was a REAL low point!

But by focusing, we were able to learn the typical problems, challenges, and obstacles that were encountered within our model. You can do the same for whichever model you choose. We learnt what questions to ask and what properties to avoid. You can, too. And when you do, you'll have MUCH less stress in your life!

In property, there are a wealth of opportunities you can take advantage of and it is very easy to get distracted. Especially if you are relatively new to property investment! It seems like there is a new opportunity popping up each week. Why on Earth would you say no to them when everyone else is doing it? You don't want to miss out!

My advice?

Let Go and Learn to Say NO!

STOP...

Take a breath...

... and LET GO.

You might already be working on a number of opportunities. That's fine, it doesn't mean you have to carry on with them all. Really think about what you want, and ask yourself what is going to serve you best as a business in the long run? Then cut out whatever you are working on (or thinking about working on) that isn't helping you achieve your goal.

If you are focusing on too many things, then in the long run it is going to be counterproductive for you and your business. Doing more doesn't lead to more. The narrower you keep that focus, the more capacity you will have to spend the time and attention on deals that are truly right for you.

Saying "No" can be painful at first, but believe me when I say you'll be happy you did in the long run. We've had some fantastic opportunities offered to us over the last few years, but they just weren't the right opportunities for us, and that is okay! There were even some that we didn't have the right clarity at first and therefore DID say "yes" to... only to subsequently realise they were a shiny penny! In these instances we would decide to walk away from them retrospectively (I can think of one example where we were over £7K into the deal on professional fees when we realised this, and we still decided to cut our losses and let go. And I'm so glad we did). Once you start learning to say "No" you'll find it is actually liberating.

You will be comfortable in the knowledge that you are so FOCUSED and DRIVEN on what you have set out to do, you don't need that extra opportunity. When you start seeing results compound as a result of your focus, saying no will become easy.

If the goal is to create more cash flow (it is!), what should you focus on? How do you create more cash flow with focus?

Nail One Model BEFORE You Diversify

Focus on one business model at a time. This enables you to set clear expectations with investors. When you understand the mechanics of how the model works from a detailed financial perspective, you can present it to investors with clarity. Clarity for investors means they are more likely to invest, which means you can line up your finance in advance of finding the deal.

With finance lined up, you can move ahead straight away with confidence when you do find a deal. No more frantically raising finance after the deal is agreed. It's in that frantic state, trying to put out fires, that we end up working with the wrong investors out of desperation!

Many people think that by choosing one business model and focusing on it, that they'll miss out on opportunities. The opposite is true. With focused intention, you get more opportunities because people know who you are and what you are doing. They bring more of the right kinds of opportunities to you because they are attracted to you.

When we focused on blocks of flats in Thanet, and became known for that, opportunities came to us. A lot of times, blocks of flats aren't listed for sale on the open market. You've got to know the right people who know what you're looking for and that you're serious. Then when they find the right opportunity for you, they will present it. One of the best deals we did in 2017/2018 was an opportunity that came to us purely because we were known as 'the people who buy blocks of flats'.

Of course, not every opportunity will be right. We had some opportunities that weren't the right price. So we would put in an offer at a price that we could do, knowing that it would probably not come to anything. Then put the deal in our pipeline (in Asana) and wait, following up every few weeks or months – waiting for the motivation of the vendor to change to be open to our offer. Which inevitably it does for a certain percentage of the offers that you put in.

You may think you are cutting out opportunities by zeroing in on one thing. But there are loads of great opportunities you're not even seeing because you aren't being intentional. By focusing on ONE model, you'll spend less time firefighting, be calmer, and make better decisions. You'll also naturally take a systemised approach, which — as you know from the last chapter — makes it easier to delegate as you grow.

When it's easier to delegate, it's easier to step back and spend your time focusing on high value, income generating tasks (IGTs). And when you focus more of your time on IGTs, you will create more cash flow in less time. That is how you do more deals, build a better business, and create consistent, life changing cash flow.

When should you diversify, then? At what point is it OK to start looking into another model? Our experience, both in our own business and working with hundreds of property investors, is that you should stick with one model MUCH longer than you think. When we showed that commercial conversion project (the one we didn't do) to our business mentor, he gave us some of the best advice we'd ever had in property. It's worth reading it again:

"You've got a great small refurb / portfolio business that is working. Something that you can sensibly scale. Why are you trying to do something else?"

Deri saved us from ourselves on that project, but I STILL wanted to do other things. I STILL chased COOL and SEXY. My ego got in the way.

Once you choose a model, then get really good at it. Property investing can help you gain a life of freedom, but to scale fast and avoid the mistakes we made (or make them less painful) choose your model and stick with it until it's successful.

Here's an acronym for FOCUS that is fitting when it comes to finding freedom:

> **F**ollow
> **O**ne
> **C**ourse
> **U**ntil
> **S**uccessful

FOCUS. Choose your model, stick with it, and scale. THAT is how you get to true freedom faster!

But the question you may be asking now is... which model should you choose?

Choose a Model to Suit Your Goals

This is KEY! I keep reassessing my goals every year with Dave – he always challenges me, and we come up with far better goals and plans because of it. The models we choose align with our goals to be able to travel, have less stress, and feel free. Sounds simple! But getting to this clarity has been so hard and has taken a huge amount of discipline.

Luckily, as 2016 came to a close we managed to mostly tame the Shiny Penny monster and found our focus again. Since then, all we've done is focus and refine. Everything we do, we look at through the lens of our goals. Everything! Doing so has allowed us to make a scalable and replicable model. Now we have systems, processes, and a team in place. Our business is not reliant on our constant involvement.

When you choose — and are clear about what you do — you also get clarity about what you *don't* do. All we do is blocks of flats in Kent.

Do we do conversions to flats? No.

Do we do developments into flats? No.

We do existing blocks of flats (between 4-15 units) on one freehold. We purchase well — they are usually in a very tired condition. Then we bring them to a good quality standard through refurbishment. After that, we rent them out long-term, refinance, and go on to the next deal.

That's it. Focusing on ONE model and refining it based on our goals gave us the fastest route to making money and, ultimately, FREEDOM.

Every time you start being drawn in by something that you think people around you will think is cool, ask yourself *is this really my fastest route to making money, or am I just being guided by my ego?*

Freedom Formula: Do More Deals

If you want to achieve financial freedom you need to build cash flow — regardless of your model. To increase cash flow, you MUST do more deals. It only works if you consistently go out and do more deals. But you can only do more deals if you have the finance available to make it happen. Which means you've got to raise finance that is compatible with the sort of deals you want to do.

To raise finance, you have to be clear about the deals you want to do so you can set expectations with potential investors. And that means taking a systemised approach — a clear, replicable model that you can do over and over again. Every time you do it, it gets easier.

Eventually, what you started with hard work becomes a machine that can keep growing without your involvement. (That's when you can look at diversifying, but not before.) In this way you can quickly grow a property portfolio that actually gives you cash flow.

So to summarise, there are three elements you need to focus on to achieve consistent cashflow and financial freedom:

1. **Do more DEALS.** Know your business model inside out so you can source appropriate deals faster and easier.
2. **Raise more FINANCE.** Be so clear about the sort of deals you do that you can articulate to potential investors how the returns work. Recognise the relationship between the deals you want to

do, the finance you need to raise, and the service that you offer to investors.

3. **Take a SYSTEMISED APPROACH.** Focus on making your process replicable so that every time you do it, it gets easier. Which means the next time you can be a little bit less involved, and the process can be quicker. Doing it this way speeds up your path to stepping back from the day-to-day in your business.

We continue to grow our portfolio by following the above steps. We also mentor other investors with the blend of both business coaching and property mentoring that Property Strategy has become known for. Our mentees do a variety of different business models, but the thread that unites them all is a replicable model to do more deals and raise more finance with a systemised approach. THAT is a laser-focused way to build cash flow.

Chapter 9

Lessons From the Worst Deal We Ever DID

Once we decided to focus on blocks of flats, we agreed three properties within a few months of moving to Margate.

The first was a standard refurb. It had four flats and required very little work. We were experienced with fairly heavy refurbs: full 1st fix and 2nd fix plumbing, re-plastering, full rewire, internal reconfiguring. We'd moved walls and added steels to support new openings. All the typical works you'd expect on refurb projects; this one included nothing new for us.

The second was a 'hybrid conversion'. There were details we hadn't foreseen.

The entire building of six flats was on a single-phase electrical supply. Every flat was tripping all the time. It was crazy. So we had to get three-phase power installed. Also, the top floor flat was unfinished when we bought the property and we hadn't known enough to ask why. It turns out the building height required either a sprinkler system or fire escape. That also meant the top floor wasn't officially a flat. So not only did we have to install a sprinkler system, but we had to do all the necessary acoustic and fire separations for a full conversion. We also had to upgrade and split the water supply. So it was somewhere between a refurb and a full conversion project.

The third property was our first full commercial conversion. Which will be forever be etched into my psyche (and still gives me a little shiver inside when I walk or drive past it!)...

After our business coach talked us out of 'the property nightmare that never was' I was still keen to give commercial conversions a go[1]. For me, commercial conversion was the pinnacle of property investing — and my ego still wanted to be that person.

Always remember that the property community loves to sell Shiny Pennies. We had done courses on commercial conversions and developments. I'd been misled by phrases like 'my builder project manages everything' and 'my planning consultant says it will be fine'.

I kept hearing, "You don't need to know all this stuff yourself. You just need a great team!"

And always there was the all-important line we kept hearing — dangled like a carrot:

"Conversions are just refurbs with more zeros on the end."

So I looked for a gateway project. A stepping stone. Something smaller. It took over a year to find it, but it was ideal. And it looked so simple.

The following section includes extracts from a book I contributed to called *Property Nightmares* by a friend of mine, Angelos Sanders. Angelos is a prolific investor in his own right, and he pulled together this series of stories from both his own experiences and from a few of his property investor friends. It's designed to act as an experience led 'training manual' for anyone wanting to get real about what it means to invest in property. If you want to avoid other peoples' pitfalls, then I highly recommend reading this book.

Still Sexy, Still Cool, Start Small, Right?

In the property investing community, when projects don't go as planned, it

1. See Chapter 5: Saying 'Yes' to Every Opportunity COSTS Time, Money, and Freedom, The Best Deal We DIDN'T Do

can be a taboo situation. You might hear whispers from other people, or through the grapevine, that things haven't really gone to plan. I'm going to be very open about what went wrong and what we wish we'd known going into the project. I felt so much shame with this project at the time, so I can understand why others don't share the challenges openly, particularly not when you are in the thick of it.

So we'll use this as some self-therapy to help me shake any remnants of shame! And to help you make more informed decisions as you move forward. This project, along with one or two others, was the biggest reason behind our decision to continue with one model and not deviate from it.

Whilst the property courses we'd done had been great and informative, in turned out we'd only scratched the surface of what we really needed to know to be successful at this. What follows is what we didn't hear about scaling up from refurbishments to commercial conversions.

Let's start with why we thought doing this project was a good idea...

It was an empty shop on the ground floor, with three floors above. The top three floors were already arranged as two flats but just needed reconfiguring to a better layout. However, none of the work had been done properly from a building regulations perspective. The plan was to convert the shop into two 1-bed flats and refurbish the two units above. Two flats and a shop converted into four flats. Simples!

But it got better:

- We could convert the commercial unit into two flats under Permitted Development (PD). The units above weren't *officially* residential. But under PD we could turn them into residential because they were above a commercial unit. This made everything simpler on the planning side and reduced planning risk.
- The project was eligible for a £25,000 per unit (£100,000 in total) interest-free "empty home loan" from the local authority. The £100,000 remained interest-free for up to three years — helping to reduce finance costs.
- Two residential units already existed in some form. In many ways that made it 50% conversion and 50% heavy refurbishment (or so we thought).

- As a commercial property, there was no 3% Stamp Duty Land Tax (SDLT) surcharge for second-home owners. This reduced our upfront costs even further.

Everything about this project made sense so we did exactly what we'd learnt on training courses: We put together a great team and got to work.

A Comedy of Errors

The following is for your benefit. Even though we can laugh about it now, at the time it was a real-life nightmare. One filled with many painful lessons.

First, there are five key areas within any commercial conversion. They are:

1. Utilities
2. Planning
3. Builders and Professionals
4. Building Control
5. Finance

If you get ONE of the five wrong, it's bad enough.

What follows is what happens when everything that can go wrong, DOES go wrong!

Enjoy!

Unbelievable Utilities

Splitting utilities is painful and expensive. It requires:

- A local supplier (e.g., Thames Water or UK Power) to upgrade the supply.
- A certified tradesman (e.g., a qualified electrician or plumber) to prepare the internal supply for the new connection.
- In the case of electricity and gas, you also need a utility company (e.g., British Gas or EDF) to connect the external supply to your internal wires and install a meter.

This project had issues with both the water and electricity supplies, but it was the electricity that caused us the biggest nightmare.

UK Power came to survey the site and confirm its requirements to upgrade the supply to the building. This part went well! Then, EDF came to confirm exactly what was needed for them to install the meters. This also went well. I had the opportunity to dig into the details of what they wanted to ensure that everything was ready.

Now we come to the real crux of the matter.

The primary issue with upgrading your electric supply is that once UK Power have installed the new supply, there is no electricity until the utility company fits the meters and connects you. If even ONE thing isn't right, they can refuse to install. Which means you are left without electricity — on a building site — until the issue is resolved!

Of course, I used a respectable and certified electrician to certify all internal works. He'd done work for us before. Also, I made sure that I'd understood *exactly* what EDF meant by 'all electrics must be at least 90% complete'. We followed their instructions to the letter, then booked two dates: One for UK Power to cut our supply, and another for EDF to install the new meters. When the big day arrived, I was quietly confident. I'd triple checked everything. We'd done everything we'd been told.

What could go wrong?

EDF arrived and within five minutes walked straight back out the door, saying that they weren't happy to install. We would need to rebook.

Apparently, we hadn't properly secured the hole where the wires exited the distribution box. I literally could NOT believe it. This was a ridiculous reason for refusing to install the meters! It could easily be resolved after the meters had been fitted. Safety first!? Why — if it was a safety rule — was the distribution box made and sold in that way? Not to mention the whole set up was legally required to be contained in a lockable electricity cupboard. Children (or adults with small hands?) shouldn't be able to access it anyway!

EDF said that once sorted, they would definitely be able to install the meters.

It was fixed within 45 minutes. Unfortunately, we couldn't book another visit for a further two weeks! During which time we were left without any electricity to the site. We almost hired an extremely expensive generator to keep the works going. Thankfully, the shop next door allowed us to run an extension cable out their back window and into our building for £10 per day. It was a tangle of wires and cables that slowed work — not something we wanted to do long-term.

The next time EDF visited they were happy with the distribution box. But it only took another two minutes to discover that we hadn't earthed our gas meters. They refused to wait for our electrician to come and do the 10-minute job and walked out.

"Once THAT is sorted, we can, 100%, DEFINITELY install the meters." Thankfully, this time we only had to wait a week.

Unfortunately things didn't get any better! The next time, they weren't happy with some of our light fittings. The time after that, it was the fireproof board the distribution box was mounted on, which they had seen every other time they visited!

On, and on, and on... it went. Always the promise of ONE MORE THING that needed fixing. And NEVER happy to wait while the problem got resolved.

In total, I had six visits by EDF over an eight-week period! Work slowed to a crawl, and we had an extra £600 in electricity costs.

Unpredictable Planning

I had always believed that if you use a great planning consultant, then you shouldn't have too many planning issues. Particularly when only needing permission under Permitted Development rights. Unfortunately, that is NOT how things went down.

The property training industry loves to collectively chant 'build a great team' like a mantra. With that in mind, we chose an extremely experienced and competent planning consultant. Even so, you can never underestimate the frustrating negligence and incompetence of local authorities.

This project required two different planning applications. The first was under permitted development rights with a turnaround of six weeks from submission. The second was full planning with a turnaround of 10 weeks from submission. I allowed for a four-week contingency to accommodate delays in the full planning application. As such, we built that delay into the schedule for any of the works associated with the full planning application. However, in the words of our planning consultant, the permitted development elements were "a sure thing".

The problems began when we contacted our planning consultant to check on our first application. The planning department was obligated to provide a ruling within six weeks from the date of submission. After that, it would be automatically granted. As far as I was concerned, this was a legally binding deadline. No chance it could be extended for any reason...

I couldn't have been more wrong!!

The planning department doesn't have an obligation to check the application and let you know if something is incorrect. And if it isn't 100% correct, then deadlines mean absolutely nothing. But surely nothing could be wrong with the application?! I'd used a highly competent and respected planning consultant!?

Four weeks after our initial submission we phoned the planning department just to check. They couldn't find ANY record of the application in their system! It took TWO WEEKS to find out what had happened. It turned out there were two different approaches we could have taken to make the two flats above the shop legal. We had chosen the WRONG one! Our application was sitting on a pile of paperwork on the wrong desk. Completely ignored!

By the time it was found, it put us back to square one. We were then told that our next application would be sped through the system due to the fact that no-one had picked up on this error. Of course, this didn't happen! We eventually received the first application back 21 weeks after initial submission — over THREE TIMES as long as the expected six weeks.

If only the delays had stopped there...

We still had the full application to get through. For this one, the planning officer wasn't happy with a couple of details such as the size of the dormer, or a bay window to the front façade. Instead of contacting us to discuss the details within the 10 weeks, they waited until the deadline and refused the application. After some back and forth over various details this application was eventually granted after 18 weeks.

But the saga didn't end...

I subsequently found that our draftsman had very kindly included various extra details within the drawings for the full application. For example, what materials we intended to use on the cheeks of the dormer, and a stylistic line of red bricks to the front façade underneath new windows.

As we all know, building works don't always go to plan. We found that the windows actually needed to bisect the red line of bricks on the front façade due to internal ceiling heights. And we'd ended up using cladding on the dormer cheeks rather than render as was noted in the plans. Due to these tiny changes (alongside various other complications) we had to make another planning application to amend the plans. Time to resolution? An additional 12 weeks!

It turns out that even with experienced planning consultants and draftsman on board, you can still have... *complications*. The planning applications for this project should have taken a total of 14 weeks to get full approval. They were simple applications with very few potential complications that could extend the timeframe. The ENTIRE PROJECT was originally supposed to be fully completed within 20 weeks! However, it took about 32 weeks from the first submission to having all permissions granted. Not something anyone needs when working with expensive bridging finance.

Bungling Builders and Procrastinating Professionals

With all builders and professionals, there is a holy triad: good quality, reliable, and affordable. In the search for this you will inevitably work with some real duds. The only thing you can do is try to engineer it so the first time you use a new trade, builder, or professional, it's on a smaller project. That way you lower your risk.

Which is exactly where I went wrong on this nightmare project!

I made the bad decision to try out a new structural engineer on the project. She seemed brilliant! Years of experience, working on well-known buildings, great references, and she could talk the talk. Most importantly (or so I thought at the time), she was well priced. To be safe, I carried out due diligence and she came through with flying colours.

Aside from the planning debacle and its effect on the timeframe, the project got off to a great start. The structural engineer felt that not much would be required to ensure our conversion of this lovely old building would be satisfactory. The problems began after about a month.

We were putting in a dormer and removing some old wooden supports in the top floor to open it up for an open plan kitchen/lounge. It was my draftsman who first mentioned the floor joists to this top floor. He asked what our engineer had said about the joists as he wasn't sure they were adequate. The engineer hadn't mentioned them at all... So, I quickly phoned. After a short discussion it was agreed that she'd come back and have another look.

Originally, the engineer had said that all we needed was one steel beam in the top room to support the roof where we were adding the dormer. Later, she decided that a second steel beam might be sensible because we were removing some wooden supports. By the end of the project, she had changed her mind again. We had to replace the entire floor with new joists and add four steel beams to support both the roof and new floor. That was four times as much steel as originally planned!

But it didn't end there...

On one of his final visits, our warranty surveyor asked us a simple question:

"What is that steel beam resting on?"

Mind you, we thought (again) that we had everything covered...

- Our fully qualified structural engineer planned and designed it.
- The beams had been fabricated and installed by a company doing this type of thing for 50 years! (And its own structural engineers were involved in the project!?)

- Our builder — both competent and experienced — helped install them.
- The building control officer had viewed the completed work and didn't find anything amiss. And...
- We had a party wall agreement with the neighbour saying the beams would be installed in his wall (signed off by a surveyor, no less).

Surely between these four experienced and competent professionals, there was no way it had been done wrong?!

It was the warranty surveyor who walked in and said "You can't do that. It's not going to support the steel. Is there a supporting wall behind it?"

We looked. Turns out he was completely right. These massive steel beams had been supported on the chimney breast rather than the party wall. Any building control officer or structural engineer knows this type of chimney breast was not suitable to act as a primary support. Absolutely no one had picked up on it. Worse, our structural engineer had told us to do it!!

The solution was not at all fun or cheap.

We had to install a £5,000, 9-meter steel beam along the ceiling of the floor below. It ran all the way from the front to the back of the building. Steel columns then ran up from that beam to support the steel beams above. The 9-meter steel had to be craned-in through a 3rd floor window in three pieces. The worst part? We had already finished all works in the floor below! We had to cut through NEW walls to fit the steel, making a massive mess. Then we had to make everything good again.

Needless to say we fired the first structural engineer. It was a new engineer and Dave who came up with the final solution – incredibly Dave was actually the one who came up with the idea! He seemed to have a way to be able to 'get' what the problems were, and to be able to think outside the box to see solutions that so often the professionals couldn't. Not only that but he was such a great communicator that he was able to put his ideas across in a way that professionals like structural engineers would considered.

The end result was approximately £25k in extra costs — extra steel, crane hire, extra design fees, making good after the steel work was completed — and a four-week delay to the project because other works couldn't continue until this was resolved.

Botched Building Control

Building Control is the UK's institutional method to ensure building works are carried out to a safe and satisfactory standard and adhere to government regulations. I had always imagined that your local building control would understand exactly what you need to do to comply. So long as you follow exactly what they tell you to do, you should be fully covered on all regulations related to structural safety, fire safety, acoustics, insulation, etc.

It turns out that couldn't be further from the truth.

In fact, in my experience your local building control can turn out to be much more of a liability than a help. So much so that if you are unfortunate enough to get an incompetent building control officer and follow their advice, you may not pass tests required to get a building control certificate. And that's if they can even be bothered to turn up to sign off your works in the first place!

That's exactly what happened in our worst-ever building control nightmare.

We (my builder and I) decided to trust and follow our building control officer's advice and specifications. This included detailed specifications on what we needed to do for fire protection/insulation, fire alarm systems, sound insulation, and thermal insulation. In fact, we just followed his advice on everything.

Around three months into the project — when we had already started finishing one of the flats — we brought around some more experienced developers to show them the project. During the tour they asked me what we'd done about sound proofing between the flats. Upon describing what our building control officer had specified, they looked incredibly surprised and a little worried.... which had me starting to feel a little worried! They gave me the number of their acoustic engineer and suggested I have a chat with him ASAP.

They had every reason to look worried. Turns out the building control officer had massively under spec'd what needed doing. The acoustic engineer made it very clear that the measures we had taken had absolutely no chance of passing the acoustic tests required for new flats. The craziest thing was that we couldn't get our building control certificate without these acoustic tests. So, by following the advice of the building control officer we had made it impossible to get building control sign off!

Worse, had we found this out at the end of the project and then had to spend tens of thousands of pounds rectifying the error, building control would have had ZERO LIABILITY for their bad guidance!

As it was, this mistake cost us about £4,000 to rectify. We had to install everything retrospectively and redo various works that were already completed. It added a further three weeks to the project!

But wait, there's more!

Turns out we had also installed the wrong fire alarm system, meaning a whole new higher grade of system had to be retrospectively installed — AFTER all works had been completed — to comply with fire safety regulations. Add another £2,500 to the total cost.

But the biggest extra cost (and stress factor) came at the very end of the project... (What? You thought that was it?)

Once we'd finished all the works, completed all tests, and complied with all regulations, we were ready. We just needed ONE MORE site visit from building control so that they could issue the completion certificate.

At this point we were coming to the end of our 12-month bridge and needed building control sign off so we could refinance onto a lower interest long-term product. We'd done everything we needed to do. This should be simple, right?

WRONG!

Building control went completely silent. They didn't answer emails, wouldn't return phone calls, wouldn't even allow me to visit them at their offices. It marks the first time I've ever been thrown out of the council offices by security! For TWO WHOLE MONTHS I couldn't get a single response. Eventually, I escalated the issue with our local councillor who escalated it to the head of building control, who finally arranged for the visit to happen. Apparently, they had just been a bit too busy!

In total, the two month delay cost us c. £5,000 in additional interest payments. The final cost of choosing to work with, and following the advice of, our local building control was an additional £11,500 on this project. Brilliant... NOT!

Frustrating Finance: An Insider's Guide to "Computer Says No" Solicitors

Banks can be a nightmare, particularly when it comes to ironing out small details and ticking all their boxes. But from my experience, the worst part of the finance process is banks' solicitors! How so?

Often banks can be reasoned with — they understand how to take a view on more unusual situations. The problem is, they also need to have the thumbs up from their own legal representation. Without it, they are at risk of potentially invalidating their insurances or violating their own borrowing conditions. This leaves you at the mercy of whichever law firm the bank has chosen to represent them. I've found that the worst lawyers are those who only see in black and white. They cannot comprehend that they might not know everything, even within areas that are nothing to do with law!

At the end of the project I was refinancing from a bridge onto a long-term product. Both products were with the same bank, so I didn't anticipate any problems. The bank had vetted everything when agreeing the bridge. Then, the unpredictable planning mess came back to haunt us.

The problems began when the bank's solicitors started asking questions about the new internal layouts. They asked why the layouts agreed in our planning permission were different to the actual internal layouts. More specifically, why was there an extra flat that hadn't been included in the submitted plans?

I wouldn't begrudge you from thinking that this was, in fact, a valid question. Without all the facts, you might think we were in breach of our planning permission. However, the bank's solicitor most certainly had EVERY fact he needed to solve this riddle himself.

To recap:

I had three different planning permissions for this project. One was under full planning and related only to the external changes. The other two were under permitted development rights related specifically to the internal layouts. The issue was that the first permitted development application was to turn the building into three flats. Six months later I realised we could fit another flat into the building. So, I applied again under permitted development rights to add a fourth flat.

Due to the change of plan halfway through, no single application had the final correct layout on it. To understand what had been granted, the solicitor needed to grasp the details of each application and know the timeline.

Not simple, but... lawyer!?

Imagine an experienced property lawyer who works primarily on commercial property cases. He has years of experience dealing with complex planning permissions. He works on behalf of a commercial bank that deals with complicated projects on a daily basis. You'd expect he'd be able to work it out, right?

For some reason, this lawyer ignored the big picture. In his opinion, the only floor plan that mattered was the one that wasn't relevant. He only cared about the floorplan that was in the application for external changes to the building — ignoring the others!

I hadn't even considered using that floorplan. It was just the first ideas drawn up by our draftsman to be able to include something in the application. And officially, those internal layouts weren't even part of the application!

We argued with this "computer-says-no" lawyer for three weeks. Our planning consultant sent several very convincing emails. The lawyer refused to relent. He stubbornly insisted that the ONLY solution was for me to make another application. Correct floor plans or no long-term finance.

In the end, I was stuck on that bridge finance for 10 weeks longer than I should have been. One obtuse lawyer cost me an unnecessary £6,000 in extra interest payments.

Cancelled Holiday and a Laundry List of Problems

There you have it, a selection of commercial conversion nightmares... from just one project! It brings me out in a cold sweat just reminiscing about them. When I share this story with mentees, it inevitably brings up a lot of questions.

Interestingly, the questions are often about specific issues. Should we have known it was better to not use local building control? Did we consider making a claim against the structural engineer's professional indemnity insurance? Should we have had the planning applications reviewed by a second planning consultant?

All valid questions, and important. But there's something more insidious with a project like this. Especially if you plan to stay in the property investing game long-term. Imagine issues with each part of a project hitting all at once. No matter how hard you work or how creative you are, the outcome is out of your control. At least, that's how it felt at the time.

- Ongoing issues with utilities and lack of power on site...
- Issues with building control and structural engineers...
- Planners who (it seemed) actively worked against us...
- The finance company approving the bridge loan, with full understanding of the project whilst...
- The "computer-says-no" lawyer refused to approve the move to a long-term product without another full planning application!

It was as if they had all joined a club and made a pact: *Let's make this project as difficult as possible!*

You might feel like you were wading through TREACLE because NOTHING and NO-ONE seemed to be on your side. The impact of a project like this on your mental wellbeing can be BIG. We experienced stress, anxiety, bad sleep, poor nutrition, and a general struggle to focus. This entire project took its toll on us.

To top it all off, we had planned a two-week holiday of a lifetime to Cape Town with my Dad during this debacle. Instead, we cancelled due to builder issues and laboured on site instead. So much for our #holidayevery6weeks lifestyle. It doesn't always go to plan!

2018: Commercial Conversion vs 4-Flat Refurb — Comparing the Numbers

Let's compare our commercial conversion nightmare with the four 4-flat refurb project we were doing at the same time. This highlights why we chose ONE model and why I suggest you do the same. At least for a while.

	Refurb	**Conversion**
Purchase Price	£330,000	£240,000
Purchase Costs	£16,000	£4,000
Refurb	£58,000	£293,000
Finance	£26,000	£63,000
Total Costs	**£430,000**	**£600,000**
Total Cash Required	£180,000	£405,000
End Valuation	£515,000	£580,000
Project Profit	**£80,000**	**- £20,000**
Cash Left In	£60,000	£167,000
Ongoing Cashflow	£1,230	£1,060
ROI on money left in	**25%**	**7.60%**

Yes you read that right, the profit on the commercial conversion was... MINUS £20,000!

GO TEAM!

If you've ever been through anything like this...

You feel your heart rate rising...

Beads of sweat forming on your forehead...

A weird mix of hot and cold at the same time...

No appetite...

Exhausted but you can't sleep because of all those compounded nightmares...

You are NOT alone.

Welcome to the Brilliant Project Club

Remember that first single let I did in 2014? We got 19% returns on the money held in from that poxy little £108,500 project. Nearly every single let we did after that had similar returns.

Dave analysed the returns on the money held in numbers comparing the commercial conversion (7.6%) to the simple heavy refurb (25%) and said "F — that! Simple refurbs are much better, easier, simpler, makes more money. Let's just scale that!"

I know that had we chosen to do another commercial conversion we could have done it better with the learnings from our first one. It definitely wouldn't have been the same. But the problem is we absolutely HATED it. We're great at value engineering things and figuring out legal structures. But this? That's not us. We followed the wrong advice. It made us feel like such idiots — like we'd failed.

The lessons we learnt were invaluable. That's why it's important to share — so others can leverage the great loss we made. And it could have been worse. I know people who have done a heck of a lot worse. It happens often with people doing their first commercial conversions, but you don't hear about it. I hear about it as a mentor, and I can promise you it happens more than you realise.

People confide in me — they book a strategy session and tell me about it. They don't share it on social media, or at property events, because there is shame. We felt that, too. There was so much shame that we didn't talk about it at the time.

The silver lining? It really WAS our university degree in how commercial conversions work and what can go wrong. Now we pass the knowledge and experience on. It also meant we could make a clear choice: We do blocks of flats. We got rid of all the planning elements. We got rid of as much building control as possible. We just took everything from the commercial conversion we didn't like and stripped it out.

Refurb I can freaking do! Add a wall? Add a bedroom? No problem. I don't want to deal with complex planning or splitting utilities. We avoid things that are out of our control. We don't enjoy it and it adds too much risk. Since then, we've been able to scale up until the present day. And it has been a very straightforward process.

That is the story of why we bang on and on about focus and just choosing a model and sticking with it. Remember, we choose every project we do, every deal, through the lens of our goals: Freedom to travel, more time, less stress. All of this was impossible during the commercial conversion.

Now I have friends who have been very successful with commercial conversions, and as a concept I think they are great. Nothing wrong with them as an investment model. And after this one, we could have said, "Great learning, let's go do another one and not mess it up this time." But it just didn't align with our goals.

So, instead, we said "Let's do something simpler that does align with our goals."

It was a very key moment.

Freedom Formula: Competence and the Dunning-Kruger Effect

When you learn anything new, there's something called the Hierarchy of Competence. Some call it the Four Stages of Competence. They look like this:

1. **Unconscious Incompetence.** You don't know what you don't know (not knowing, or ignorance).
2. **Conscious Incompetence.** You know of something, but not how to do it (awareness).
3. **Conscious Competence.** You can do that something, but you have to think about it and focus constantly (learning).
4. **Unconscious Competence.** You do it easily. Seemingly without effort (mastery).

Somewhere between Unconscious Incompetence and Conscious Incompetence lies a cognitive bias called the Dunning-Kruger Effect. Here's how it works...

Imagine you've learned how to buy single let flats, refurbish them, get positive cash flow, and then remortgage. Now, imagine you are learning about all these different, sexy, and cool property strategies (like we did!). And then imagine you hear from a property investment 'guru' that commercial conversions are like refurbs, but with more zeros on the end, and, therefore, more money to be made.

So, with all the confidence in the world, you overestimate your abilities, jump in, and realise too late — and quite painfully — that you don't know what you don't know.

This is the Dunning-Kruger effect, a cognitive bias where people with limited competence in a particular domain overestimate their abilities due to their lack of knowledge. Our nightmare commercial conversion was the classic example.

We'd been studying how to do commercial conversions for two years. TWO YEARS! Yet, when we finally got there, we hadn't scratched the surface of what we needed to know. We expected it to be hard. What we didn't expect was the shame (again, this isn't shared in the industry) of making so many mistakes.

But we also didn't expect the numbers to look so bad that, along with the stress of the project, it didn't make any sense for us to keep doing commercial conversions when we could do tired blocks of flats, grow our portfolio, and be FREE.

Much faster. Much easier. Less stress.

Chapter 10

How Holiday Every Six Weeks Became a Reality

Our work with Elliot in 2015 had been a game changer because it made us realise how important time off, holidays and travel were for us. Yes, Financial Freedom was important, but our priority was TIME freedom. This was different to many of the people we were hanging out with, who were much more financially motivated. Reconnecting with why we started, and focusing on creating more Time Freedom, really started to change how we made decisions.

At that time we were working every hour under the sun, spinning so many different plates, that it felt like we'd sold our souls to property! There was no longer a difference between evenings or weekends... it was just work, work, work!

We focused on changing our mindset about time, and work. We started to realise that by working all the time, we were actually less productive and making worse decisions. We couldn't see the wood for the trees anymore! The decision to change this was easy, but actually *doing* it was hard. It was like being addicted to chocolate and trying to wean yourself off it. But we knew it was of paramount importance. So even though there was a powerful urge to keep pushing and working all the time, we kept reconnecting with our Vision, our 'reason why', and committed to it.

A Glimmer of Hope

We started getting our evenings back! We'd leave the phones in a different room after 6:30 p.m. and prioritise time cooking a lovely meal together. We decided to stop working on Sundays, and made time for bike rides and spending time with family again. We were still working hard most of the time... but the time not working was a glimmer of hope. Like a ray of sunshine on a cloudy day. We could see the light... it was possible to make time for ourselves again!

Once this started to work, we started to think more about trying to make this #holidayevery6weeks thing happen. Once we'd broken the habit and addiction, it was surprisingly easy to not work all the time! Maybe it could be the same on the holidays front. We started to wonder how we could logistically prioritise holidays and make it happen...

Well, now it seems obvious to me, but at the time it was a revelation... We needed to get one of those big year planners and plan out how 2016 was going to work...

Pink Is for Holidays!

At the time, we were still living in South-East London. I remember sitting down with Dave at our kitchen table for the first time, getting the big A1 wall planner laid out in front of us, with lots of those small coloured sticky dots.

We decided what the different colours would represent. One colour for when Dave had concerts (he was still a professional musician at the time), another for when I was going to property training courses. There was a colour for friends and family events. And I'd just started getting booked as a speaker so there was a colour for that, as well.

Once all those 'immovable' things were mapped out over the year with different colours, we started to look where the gaps were. Where were we going to fit in more holidays?! And we chose that all important holiday colour... pink! We worked our way through all of those beautiful pink stickers mapping out the whole of 2016... when we wanted to go on holiday, and where we might go.

At that point there was not a lot of money for holidays, so most of them were simple and low budget... but we really didn't care! The fact we were starting to prioritise more time to travel, no matter how frugally, was what mattered.

We believed that if we set up this framework for holidays, and started doing the simple ones now, in the future they could become more expensive as the business grew.

In 2016, we went skiing (Courchevel La Tania again!) and ate a lot of packed lunches on the slopes to save money. We attended a friend's wedding in France and found some decent budget Airbnbs to stay in. We visited and stayed with family in Cyprus twice with some of those 'memorable' sleazyjet 'red eye' flights to keep costs down. We even had a camping trip to the New Forest.

Simple, budget... none of them longer than 7-10 days. And we absolutely LOVED IT!

Now at this time, when we were off on 'holiday' we were, in fact, still working in the business. We couldn't switch off completely at that point because the whole business was totally on us. We (mostly) didn't mind this though. The fact that we were able to regularly go away and work remotely from different locations felt like huge progress.

A Silver Lined Cloud

During the Summer of 2016, Dave had to step back from most of his work as a professional musician due to an issue with his left hand that was making it impossible for him to play. For a professional musician, this is pretty devastating. It was his life and passion. But ever the optimist, Dave saw the positive: Without this commitment, and no longer restricted by concerts and rehearsals, it became a lot easier to book holidays whenever we wanted.

As we've experienced time and time again, what feels really bad or devastating at the time, can ultimately turn out to be one of the best things that ever happens to us... and this was no exception. With Dave no longer working as a musician, and me free from employment, it gave us the freedom to up sticks and move to Margate in the Autumn of 2016.

As you know, that was a really important decision for us and our business.

When we came to doing our 2017 year planner, we were doing it in Margate! We were looking to the year ahead and planning out our holidays and time, excitedly discussing what holidays we wanted to do over the coming year!

The Best JV We Ever Did

At the end of 2016 we got married (after 13 years together), and 2017 got off to a great start with a two-week honeymoon in Malaysia! The rest of the holidays that year were simple and low cost like the year before... apart from the two-week trip to South Africa we planned for the Autumn (which as you know ended up being cancelled due to having to go and labour on site instead!).

We also had support from some team members, which made it more viable for us to switch off for longer periods during these holidays.

This was the year that also saw us start to really get our working hours under control. The work in the evenings had long been banished, and we had not only gotten our weekends back, but we were starting to move towards not working Fridays! We started to see Friday as a 'flex' day... We would plan not to work, but if an opportunity presented itself that we wanted to take advantage of, then we could make the choice to work Friday. But always with the confidence to know it would still not mean working at the weekends.

Every year we repeated the same process:

- Reconnect with our Vision, usually making a few tweaks.
- Decide what part of the Vision we wanted to prioritise next (e.g., longer holidays, more expensive holidays, fewer working hours, more exercise, more time with family and friends, eating healthier, etc.).
- Get a year planner and map out the next year to bring that priority to life.

- Once the year planner was filled out, I'd transfer it to the online calendar, blocking it out so that if we were asked to do something during a planned holiday week… we would just say no.

It was a constant evolution! In fact, it still is today as we work towards our current goal of one month on, one month off. We're always looking for the next step in the right direction towards it, knowing that it can't be rushed.

Quality of Life: Small Things Make a Massive Difference

During 2017, we continued to prioritise Time Freedom over Financial Freedom. We found that often it was the 'small things' in life that really made a massive difference to the quality of our lives. For example, time to go and run along the beach in the morning or to have a long weekend at a spa. We prioritised the 'easy wins', and pushed the more expensive parts, such as more luxury holidays, to the future. We would often make the choice to hire a new team member and take smaller pay increases as the portfolio grew to make that happen.

From 2017, until COVID hit in 2020, we were doing more and more overseas holidays - getting some two-week holidays in alongside mostly one-week ones. And the amount of time skiing kept expanding! In 2018, we skied for four weeks, in 2019, six weeks… and in 2020, we'd planned 10 weeks! (Not that COVID allowed that to play out in the end!)

Not only that, but we were learning how to switch off and disconnect more from the business when we were on holiday. The team was growing, and whilst we still had a lot to learn about how to delegate well, this support made it easier to switch off for longer periods of time. It was imperfect and messy. Sometimes we had to work more than we wanted whilst we were away, but generally with each holiday we got better at it.

The amazing thing was, the more we managed to go on holiday, and the better we got at switching off our brains, the more productive we were when working! We just seemed to have way more space and clarity to see where we were making our lives harder and to question our decisions.

As you can see, ever since setting our #holidayevery6weeks goal with Elliot back in 2015, we have continually adjusted our strategy to make it a reality.

This process has evolved into one of the most important techniques I've learned to be able to achieve Time Freedom.

Freedom Formula:
Making #holidayevery6weeks Happen

Step 1: Create Your Vision for Your Ideal Life

Key Questions to Ask Yourself

Start by taking yourself forward in time 10 years. Imagine that everything has panned out exactly how you wanted. Now, imagine what your IDEAL LIFE would look like:

- How many hours per week / month do you want to be working on your business?
- What will you spend your free time doing? (Ideas: holidays, family, friends, hobbies, giving back, gym, family meals...)
- How often do you want to be doing these things? (i.e., How many times per week do you want to go to the gym? How many holidays do you want? What hobbies will you pursue?)

Be really SPECIFIC and DETAILED when you answer these questions.

Dream BIG

Aim for your idea of perfection. This may be hard to do, but challenge yourself because this is the first step to creating your Ideal Lifestyle and making it a reality. It may seem a million miles away from the life you are living now... That is OK!

Step 2: Decide Your Priorities

What aspects of your ideal life do you want to prioritise making a reality first? Choose 2-3 MAX.

Now, you don't just keep your head down and work really-hard for 10 years, and then one day magically wake up to this amazing life you've dreamed up. It's a gradual process towards making your life work this way OVER the next 10 years. As you have just read, I didn't go from working 80 hours a week with no holidays planned, to suddenly going on holiday every 6 weeks, having all weekends and evenings off, cooking lovely dinners with Dave 3-4 times per week, and getting to the gym 3 times per week. Far from it! I started small – I started by MAKING TIME for half an hour of NAIL PAINTING each week, and then layered on the other elements step-by-step.

Once you've written down your ideal life, choose a few elements from it to begin prioritising straight away, and decide your first step to making it happen.

For example: Gym Time

- Ideal: 'Go to the gym every day'.
- Currently: You are not doing any exercise at all.
- First step: Go to the gym once a week, every week (until it becomes a habit).
- Second step: Once step one is complete, expand to go to the gym two to three days a week (until it becomes a habit).
- Continue layering on the next level of progress towards your goal, step-by-step, until you are going to the gym every day!

Step 3: Time Blocking to Make Space for What's Important

We start with high-level time blocking: What's our vision? How are we going to achieve it? We block that out on an annual basis. Get that yearly wall planner and map out all the big things that you want to have time for, and choose when you're going to do them.

Once you are happy with it, then transfer it over to an online calendar. There you can easily refer to it on a day-to-day basis when deciding whether to say 'yes' to something that may clash with a holiday, or something else important to you.

Then you can get more granular, time-blocking on a week-to-week basis as you move through the next steps. Remember, time blocking is something that is an iterative process. It requires commitment to do it, regularly checking where it's not working, and then adjusting accordingly. You will also have to find the right balance in terms of how detailed you get. If you time block your whole life out straight away, it's probably going to be too much and you won't honour it. Take it step-by-step and layer it up and improve it over the weeks, months and years ahead. This is a marathon, not a sprint.

Step 4: Cascade Priorities from Your Vision to Your Week

You are clear about your Vision, but that's a massive idea looking many years in the future, and it's not that helpful to guide your current, day-to-day priorities. So we want to break it down into 'bitesize' chunks.

This is probably one of the things in my 'genius zone' — one of the things I do really well. I'm always clear WHAT the priority tasks are, and then get them DONE!

Looking at your Vision, what is the first big step towards that in the next year? This is your Annual Goal. Then based on your Annual Goal, what are the next steps to take to move in that direction over the next quarter (3 months)? And we continue breaking it down like this right down to the WEEK. It looks like this:

1. **VISION:** Start here - where do you want to be in 10 years' time?
2. **ANNUAL GOAL:** From your Vision, what is the goal over the next 12-months? What do you want to achieve this year that will take you a big step toward your vision?
3. **QUARTERLY PRIORITIES:** What are the 3-5 biggest priorities to take you towards your Annual Goal over the next 3 months? These are 3-5 mini projects to work on or improve to move in the direction of the Annual Goal. For example: Improve my investor pipeline process so that I have funds lined up for deals before I have an offer accepted.

4. **MONTHLY ACTIONS:** If those are my quarterly priorities, what do I have to get done this month to take the next step towards getting these projects completed? What 3-5 key actions do I need to take this month to move me toward my Quarterly Priorities?
5. **WEEKLY PRIORITIES:** Based on your Monthly Actions, what do you need to do this week? Again, 3-5 smaller tasks that will take you a step closer to completing your Monthly Actions.

Don't do the whole year at once, just focus on the next steps in the right direction. I don't recommend deciding your yearly priorities for the next 10 years now, just focus on the next ONE YEAR. Same with the Quarterly Priorities – just focus on the next three months. Then in three months' time, you can look back at how you did before deciding what the next priorities need to be.

Always think one step removed. What do I have to do to get myself there? Then, rinse and repeat every week, month, quarter and year. "Cascade" your priorities from your Vision, step-by-step right the way down to your week. This is what I mean by the Cascade of Priorities.

I've found this to be the best balance between being clear on your next steps so you can focus, and not wasting a ton of time planning out ALL the steps to get you from where you are now to your Vision. It's just too much to try and do in one go, and if you get too fixated on the exact route you think you're going to take, you'll end up missing opportunities and short-cuts to getting there.

Of course, you can't just *write* priorities. You've got to actually get them done! In business, there are SO many different things to get done and it's EASY to get distracted, especially in this day of social media and the overflowing inbox. This means you end up focusing on the urgent operational tasks, rather than the strategically important business growth tasks.

The Cascade of Prioritisation

And if you're like me, and you like things to be organised and perfect, it's very easy to focus on low-value tasks. For example, responding to or tidying up emails. Or filing documents. Is that really the highest value task in your business? What truly important thing is not getting done whilst you spend your time cleaning up your desktop? If you haven't already read the book *Eat that Frog* by Brian Tracey, then check it out. It's all about doing the high value tasks FIRST, because they will make the biggest difference.

For me, getting clear about priorities (as described above) and blocking in time in the weekly calendar to get them done has been essential. But it goes deeper to ensure you can remain focused during your time blocks:

3 Top Tips to Silence Distractions and Get Jobs DONE

1. **Turn off phone notifications.** Be ruthless with this. Turn ALL your notifications for social media and news apps OFF to avoid getting unnecessarily distracted throughout the day.
2. **Prioritise your most important tasks for the week.** Clearly set out your top priorities in some type of task management software (e.g., Asana or Trello). Then, block out specific times in your diary to get them completed.
3. **Time block for smaller tasks too!** Set a specific time of day to answer messages and emails. I find this is better to do at the end of the day rather than in the morning. That way I can focus on getting through my task list first.

You may want to let others know that you aren't available 24/7. In this crazy world of *instant gratification*, people sometimes seem to expect you to drop everything and reply straight away unless you tell them otherwise. You can try setting up a standard 'out of office' reply. Or, if you have an assistant, task them with doing the quick follow-up with whoever wants your time and attention. There are very few small tasks that can't wait.

Having focused pockets of time means you can get through your task list more efficiently. You'll find you start getting MUCH more done in a day once you start doing this! And once you can get a lot done in one day... you don't have to work so many days to make massive progress... meaning you get both the extra holiday time AND you do more deals!

Of course, it doesn't always go to plan; things can overrun, or I might have low energy on any given day. On those days, I just move the things I've not completed to another day (or week!) in the diary and re-prioritise them. I hold myself accountable, but I also know it won't be perfect and to give myself a break sometimes when I don't manage everything I planned to.

I know it sounds like such a free and easy, carefree thing to be doing, to go on #holidayevery6weeks – but as you can see here, there is a lot of structure, planning and discipline that's gone into making it a reality. Structure really gives you freedom I promise you! Try out what I've outlined here but make it your own so that you feel it's really YOUR structure as that will make it much more enjoyable for you.

You will get pulled in a lot of different directions as you grow your business, but having these routines and structures in place helps to ground you and to build momentum towards your end Vision.

Chapter 11

How to Grow On the Go

Once we reached our #holidayevery6weeks goal, I realised I wanted to expand it further. My original dream was to be able to go skiing for as long as I wanted to without having to ask for permission! Even the desire to leave my J-O-B hinted at something deeper. What I craved was the freedom to be wherever in the world I wanted, whenever I wanted. I call this Location Freedom, and it was the natural evolution of our initial drive to have more holidays. So it seemed only right to start planning towards doing a whole ski season! But to achieve it we needed a more structured business setup.

What follows are a few of the small steps we took, and early successes, towards achieving complete location freedom.

Season Pass!

Long before I began Tomes Homes and Property Strategy, I made plans to work as a chalet maid! Those plans got lost in a sea of working and studying, but the dream never left me.

Then, in 2013, I made that fateful decision to create a life of freedom. A life where I didn't have to dread going back to a J-O-B on Monday after a week in the French Alps. In 2016, it finally happened.

It was the first magical ski holiday where I didn't have to ASK FOR PERMISSION!! Thanks to property, I'd quit my job. Whilst this ski holiday was still short (just a week), I didn't get that sinking feeling in the pit of my stomach when we had to head home.

Two years later it got even better...

Our First Ever Season Pass — French Alps 2018

This was the magic moment...

Season pass, Les 3 Vallées, French Alps, 2018

It. Was. AMAZING!

We had four whole weeks of skiing that year. We didn't spend the entire time on holiday, but working from the slopes definitely felt like a close second! And I must admit — I cried with joy! We'd finally lived up to our promise. All the hard work, sacrifice, and stress was paying off! By the end of the trip, our car was completely buried in snow. It took about an hour to dig out. We've since come to appreciate digging a car out of the snow as a sign that we've been skiing for just the right amount of time!

Not only was it a dream come true, our season in the Three Valleys helped us begin to cut the cords from the parts of our business we don't enjoy doing ourselves.

The First Deal We Didn't Negotiate

One big step we took during this time was around negotiating property deals. Dave is amazing when it comes to analysing the small details and getting the best out of the team in the operations side of the business. I was becoming really great at looking after the business strategy, marketing our business, hiring team members and making sure we were continually writing up and delegating processes. But negotiating property deals? Dave and I hate it. It's not our strong point. For a while we had been scratching our heads, asking *how can we get out of having to negotiate deals ourselves? Who can we get to do this for us?*

When you finally choose to step back from some part of your business, there are two requirements:

First, find someone good at it.

My dad is an AMAZING negotiator. And, whereas I'm happy to sit behind my laptop all day, my dad is MUCH more of a people person. He is what's known as a Star / Supporter if you're familiar with *Wealth Dynamics* profiles (check out Recipe for Freedom below!). It took a long time for him to come to mind because he was living in South Africa at the time. I knew he was a great negotiator, but I wondered *how can you negotiate from South Africa?*

We decided to try it anyway, and he became our main negotiator for property purchases. And he managed to do it without visiting a single agent for the entire first year!

Second, put a process in place.

In this case, it was simple: First we would do the analysis, then we'd let Dad know our max offer price, then we let him get on with it. He'd just go back and forth with them until everyone was happy. (Not every process you hand off to a team member will be this clean, but occasionally there are nice simple ones like this that are easy to delegate.)

There was another (unforeseen) benefit to my dad negotiating for us. Once he moved back to the UK, he started going to see agents in person. Whilst I had been going around to agents for years, every time I met a new agent it was like starting over. Why? Well apparently, I 'don't look like the sort of person who's going to buy blocks of flats'. It just made building credibility difficult with new agents.

But my dad? He looks the part! In his own words, he's got the wise "grey hairs"! Whilst he is NOT buying blocks of flats, he LOOKS like a guy who wants to buy blocks of flats. It worked really well for us as the estate agents took him more seriously and we got more leads coming through because of it. At first, we paid him commissions and that evolved into us paying him a fixed fee for every deal successfully negotiated. Win-win.

We were actually skiing down the slope when the offer was accepted on the first deal we didn't negotiate ourselves. It was a block of four flats in Margate. Needless to say, we headed straight to the nearest alpine bar and raised our glasses to that success!

Cheers to the first deal we DIDN'T negotiate ourselves!

Recipe for Freedom:
Wealth Dynamics

Wealth Dynamics is a psychometric profiling test for entrepreneurs. Created by Roger Hamilton, it is based on the work of Carl Jung combined with elements of ancient Chinese philosophy. It's great for understanding yourself and where you are in your flow, and also has been amazing for us when it comes to growing a team that really works.

We've recorded two podcast episodes going into how we use this – one for understanding it for yourself, and another for using it to grow a team:

- In episode 30, *'Flow' or 'Oh no': understanding yourself using Wealth Dynamics*, Dom and I discuss how Wealth Dynamics can help you to gradually love what you do more and more, which is very important if you aren't in a business built from passion.
- In episode 46, *Building your Dream Team: getting your team in the right roles*, Dave and I share how to use Wealth Dynamics to build high-performing teams that excel in their roles and thrive in your business.

Check out these and our other Property Lifestyle Mastery podcast episodes at: www.property-strategy.com/podcast

2018 also saw another big milestone for Tomes Homes...

How to Close a £1 Million Property Deal from the French Alps

This one was a nail biter, but what a day! We'd set a date to exchange contracts, and everything was ready to go. All we needed to do was transfer the deposit by the next day. The key for us had been specifically choosing a bank that would allow us to transfer large sums over the phone without having to go into branch. So we weren't worried. However, something happened when Dave sent the CHAPS payment. Once the payment was approved, the bank said something like 'It *should* be two hours, but it could take up to 24'.

This was the block of 11 flats that we were buying for £1.2M with a market value of £1.5M — not a deal we wanted to lose:

Our first £1M+ purchase!

There we were, in a taxi hurtling down the mountain on our way to the airport, trying to sort out this £120k deposit. Meanwhile... the vendor was threatening to pull out if we didn't exchange that day!

Dave was on the phone with the bank saying, "It needs to be NOW or else he's going to pull out!" Eventually, the bank suggested that if we sent the payment via BACS, it was more likely to arrive on time because it didn't have to go through the same processes. But we'd already sent the money via CHAPS! Thankfully we were able to quickly pull together the money to send ANOTHER £120k via BACS transfer to ensure the funds arrived in time.

In the end, both payments arrived in time and the deal went ahead as planned, but I'll never forget that taxi journey. Needless to say, there are moments when buying property whilst travelling can be interesting!

Mini-printers, Friends in Bars, and Navigating Foreign Post Offices

There are certain practicalities that regularly come up when buying property whilst travelling. I often hear people use them as reasons for why you can't travel the world like we do. The question is, how do you actually do all the necessary things to complete deals? In particular, how do you get all those important legal documents signed, witnessed, and posted back?

Well this one's simple... you buy a travel-sized mini-printer. We bought one for around £100 that folds up and is smaller than a shoe box. We've been using the same one for years and it has made its way around the world with us: the Maldives, South Africa, all around Europe, Asia... Wherever we go! It's easy: Set it up and you're ready to print.

Once you've printed your mortgage offer, deed of charge, and personal guarantees, then you just find an unsuspecting foreigner in a bar, make friends with them, and ask them to witness it. This has been the cause of many very funny conversations with random people over the years. We've had documents witnessed by bar staff, hotel receptionists, and cleaners. We've even accosted random hotel guests whilst they're having a drink, and it makes for some interesting conversations! Then you either find a random post office (if you're in a country with a good postal service), or book a DHL collection if you're somewhere like South Africa. We've done this over and over again and it definitely keeps our lives spicy!

Blizzard!

One of our most memorable trips to the post office was when we were skiing in La Tania in Courchevel. Dave printed a set of Personal Guarantees, got someone in a bar to witness it, and off we went to the post office. But to get there, we had to take three ski lifts to get to the top of the valley and then ski down to the bottom where the post office was. When we started the weather was fine, but during ski lift number three, the weather turned. By our final run, we could NOT see where we were going, it was deep snow, and the only way down was a very difficult black run!

I'm happy to say both us and the Personal Guarantees survived, but it was one hell of an adventure on the mountain to make it happen!

Twice Is Nice

Here's a tip if you want to lower the stress levels a bit. Always post two sets of signed paperwork. Sometimes documents get lost in the post (or by the bank's solicitors). So we always make two copies of everything, post one set to the bank, and another to a member of the team in the UK (interesting how this second version always seems to arrive safely, isn't it?!).

Chapter 12

The Mortgage Offer and Downval Debacle

Coming out of the back of the commercial conversion issues, we ran into trouble with the bank.[1]

We've already covered the difficulty we had getting from our bridge financing to a long-term product on that project. Well, this is the other side of that, after we'd satisfied the bank's solicitor and they had finally ticked all the boxes related to planning. Now all we needed was the bank to make a mortgage offer.

What follows is something that every property investor faces at some point in their career. The question is, how do you deal with it?

In case you are new to property investing, here's a little context. A downval (down valuation) is when a surveyor assesses a property and says it's worth less than you had previously estimated.

For example, let's say you have a property on the market and a potential buyer makes an offer. You agree to the offer. But when the bank's surveyor assesses the property, it comes in at a lower valuation. The bank then offers a mortgage at the lower valuation. For the deal to complete, either the buyer has to come up with the difference (i.e., increase the deposit), or the seller

1. Chapter 9: Lessons From the Worst Deal We DID Do

has to lower the price. Not fun. And when it happens regularly, it can put shackles on the property market.

For property investors... it can be devastating.

So, you've raised finance for your deal, and done a refurb, development, conversion... whatever your model. You're experienced and know your market and area like the back of your hand. You're confident in your figures and end values, and you may even have a strong relationship with your bank, with promises made regarding how much they'll lend you. Then you go to refinance — to release your investors' money — only to find the bank's surveyor is hell-bent on a lower valuation! This is exactly what happened to us in 2018. But not just on one property — at this time we needed three mortgage offers on properties with a combined value of around £2M.

Three for Three

We had finally finished work on the three projects in Margate — the four flat heavy refurb, the six flat hybrid conversion, and the full commercial conversion. Off we went to our primary bank. They had given verbal assurance — promises as far as we were concerned — of mortgages at certain valuations.

So our first challenge was when we received back our Royal Institution of Chartered Surveyors (RICS) Red book valuations for all three projects. None of them were as high as expected, and one in particular had been badly down valued, coming in at about £200,000 lower than we thought it should (from our very detailed comparable property analysis!). However, the other two were in the range of our 'worst case scenario' on our deal analysis, and we quickly made a new plan to deal with the reduced amount of cash being released.

Due to all the challenges with planning, the structural engineer, and builders, the projects had overrun. Two of the three were on high-interest bridging loans. So whilst we still had a few months of our term left, we really needed to get long-term mortgages and release investors' money. Fast. The clock was ticking to get those loans repaid. But then the weeks went by with no sign of our mortgage offers! By the time we finally received them, we had been waiting for eight weeks after the valuations had come back.

We all know you need banks — they are an essential part of the property investment equation. But it is a love/hate relationship — Dave and I love and hate banks in equal measure. In this case it was more hate than love. Because when these mortgage offers finally did come through, they were for the wrong freakin' amount of money!?

The Bank Had Us Over a Barrel

We had been down valued again, but this time not by the valuer. This time it was by the bank — and it wasn't a small amount.

We had been dropped from 75% loan-to-value (LTV) down to 66% LTV. For no reason. Without warning! Considering the recent down valuations, it was a LOT of money (close to £400k between the 3 deals)!! There we were with three different deals — all blocks of flats — and a huge amount of investment not getting released.

I remember Dave on the phone during our ski trip, 'debating' with the business development manager at the bank, as always doing an incredible job at keeping cool under pressure, whilst attempting to convince them to honour their previous promises. Eventually, it took some carefully worded emails and LinkedIn messages to "the powers that be" to get a meeting booked in with people with real authority within the bank, so that we could argue our case.

After a very stressful meeting, they finally agreed to honour their promises and issue new mortgage offers at the higher LTV. However, it took three months to get our new offers issued at the right amounts (on top of the two months we had already waited for the original mortgage offers). The entire process ruined our headspace. We were in shock at what had happened, and it massively knocked our confidence and belief in property as a whole. It slowed our business growth to a snail's pace, because we couldn't focus on new deals and investors while this was all going on. We felt like we were really letting down our investors, and it didn't matter that the problems were completely out of our control, we still blamed ourselves for it.

The constant stress eventually took its toll.

Five by Two

The mortgage offer fiasco had hit me hard, especially coming off the back of the commercial conversion nightmare. I started getting classic stress-related symptoms and got ill five times in two months. First, there was a stomach illness... then flu-like symptoms... then a rash. They just kept coming, one after the other. Stress is a built-in fact of life for many business owners. The problem is that when we experience stress, our bodies release a hormone called cortisol.

Cortisol is like the body's alarm system. It plays a role in many stress-related responses. For example, that boost of energy you get when dealing with a stressful situation. Or, when you struggle with sleep or wake up early due to stress. Once the stress passes, your cortisol level *should* go back to normal along with the systems it affects. However, if stress is an underlying condition — always on — your body gets used to it. There comes a point where your body has had so much cortisol, it starts to expect more. Eventually, it catches up with you.

A New Door Opens

When Dave and I lived in London, regular visits to a chiropractor helped me to deal with chronic back pain. So not long after we moved to Margate I went in search of a new chiropractor. What I found in Stacey Rochelle — officially a chiropractor — is someone with an incredible wealth of knowledge across so many different areas of holistic health.

As we came out of the commercial conversion hell and into the stressful downval debacle, I mentioned my string of illnesses to Stacey. I've always been one to push, and push, and ignore what my body is trying to tell me. I had always thought *just take some painkillers, or if needed get antibiotics when you get sick, and then just keep pushing through.* So when Stacey introduced me to the idea that my body was reacting to the stress, it was almost like someone turned a light on!

Ultimately, you can destroy your body in the process of growing a business. Stacey helped me to start making connections I hadn't even considered. She has become an incredible force for good in both my life and Dave's life. She opened the door to us taking a holistic approach to health that continues to shape our lives and business to this day. Stacey became what feels to me like one of my guardian angels – a bright light during a dark time.

One very important lesson that Stacey continues to drive home for me is that you can't be in a constant state of stress and also improve your health. Something has to give. To improve your health and function at your best, you have to look at ways of reducing your stress levels.

Freedom Formula: Stress, Your Health, and Your Business

When we talk about stress and health with our mentees, it is fascinating. There's often a collective sigh of relief. It is as if they can FINALLY talk about their experiences without the pretence. We hear all about the different ways they attempt to deal with the stress of building a business.

Strictly speaking, this is not a self-help or personal development book. And there are A LOT of options out there. My intention is to share what we went through and give back some of what we've learned. New ways of thinking. New ways of acting. Practical ideas to help you avoid the mistakes we made.

Below are a few things to consider about stress, your health, and your business:

Acceptance Is the First Step

This might sound obvious, but so many people either don't, or won't accept that underlying stress is affecting them. Assuming you want freedom, at some point you have to accept there is stress around your property business. If you don't, it WILL catch up with you. Burnout, breakdowns, stress induced depression... they are all avoidable but ONLY if you accept that stress is a reality (even if you are calling it by a different name!). Once you do that, it's MUCH easier to say *OK, maybe the way I'm working is not working for me.*

Health Is An Extended Project

If you try to make too many big changes at once, it lowers your chance of success. You can't force yourself into a state of health. If you try, it only acts to INCREASE STRESS! Start by paying attention to your emotions and what your body is trying to tell you. Then, over time, make small changes. You'll be amazed at how well this works.

One Size Does NOT Fit All

There is SO much advice out there, it can be overwhelming. All you have to do is open social media or YouTube to see it: "Do this! THIS WORKS!" Before you decide to try something new to lower stress and increase your health, figure out how it will fit into your life.

Start by asking yourself three questions:

1. Which stresses in my life can I control?
2. What am I willing to change?
3. What actions am willing to take to change it?

Be honest with yourself and be realistic. Remember, you can't change everything at once.

Try Simple Solutions

Complicated isn't necessarily better. And we just LOVE to make things complicated. Sometimes it is as simple as taking an Epsom salt bath (one of my favourites!) or walking on grass with bare feet (usually called Earthing or Grounding). Other times, you might just need more sleep or 15-minutes of yoga in the morning.

Embrace Complexity

That might sound like a contradiction. But just as over complicating makes things worse, you also need to understand that stress is a complex issue. Dave and I continue working with Stacey to this day. (On average we saw her two to three times a month from 2017-2020! Nowadays we see her about once per quarter.) We are in great shape compared to 2017, but we still have challenges. The difference is, we're able to deal with them much quicker than before. We have tools to help us thrive through challenge rather than just survive, and ultimately they keep us energised and free from sickness.

If you'd like to know more about Stacey Rochelle (amazing lady!), check out the podcast episode we did together:

In episode 30, *From Stress to Success: healthy body & business with Stacey Rochelle,* we delve into the fascinating world of holistic health, stress management, and the interconnectedness of physical and mental well-being.

The Property Lifestyle Mastery Podcast

I've already mentioned our Top-10 Charting podcast with synopses of relevant episodes, but haven't properly introduced it!

Property Lifestyle Mastery is a labour of love where we have open conversations about what it's like to build a property business that creates cashflow and Freedom. We share the highs, the lows, and the lessons we've learned along the way, and we have some amazing conversations with those who have been instrumental to our success.

Check it out here: www.property-strategy.com/podcast

Chapter 13

From Cocky to Cooped Up

In March 2020, we were skiing again in the French Alps, back at our favourite resort La Tania, where our property journey began. We had planned TEN WEEKS of skiing this year in total — the Location Freedom was really escalating!

This was just before the world went mad with COVID. It had already spread from China. The first wave had hit Italy and by March, it had spread to every region. On March 8, Italy announced its first regional lockdown, which included the Italian Alps. By the next day, all of Italy was in lockdown.

Our friends and family urged us to return to the UK.

"Quick, lockdown is coming! You've got to get back to the UK now before this COVID thing comes!"

At this point, France was saying it would DEFINITELY not close the ski slopes. What should we do? Well obviously, we chose to stay! We felt cocky having made the superb choice to ski in the French Alps, where there clearly wouldn't be a lockdown like in Italy.

It was a mere six days later that we were having a lovely dinner at our local restaurant, feeling very smug with ourselves, when the news hit that the

French authorities had changed their minds! And we found ourselves locked down like the rest of the world!

COVID Lockdown in the French Alps

French Alps, March 2020: Lockdown Begins

That was our view as the lockdown started — at least while snow remained on the ground. We couldn't ski because they'd closed the ski lifts (it actually made me wish I'd become a cross country skier!). It was me, Dave, and about eight other people in this entire ski resort for the whole of the French lockdown. It was surreal. We watched the snow melt from our balcony.

Still, we enjoyed ourselves...

Melting Snow and Michelin Star Takeaways

As it started warming up — and Dave became bored — he got the great idea to use the ski slope in new and wonderful ways!

Ski Slope Driving Range

For his birthday, we had a golf club and some balls shipped over from the UK and Dave started hitting balls up the slope every day.

During this time we also ate very well. Our apartment was directly above a Michelin starred restaurant. Remember when so many restaurants shifted to takeaway-only service to survive COVID lockdowns? Well, these guys followed suit, and very soon there was a regular queue of cars outside our window, grabbing their Michelin Star takeaways – lucky us, we only had to pop downstairs to collect our own gourmet meals!

So, as spring arrived, it was all Michelin star takeaways, golf, and barbecues.

I had never visited the French Alps in the spring. It wasn't even on my radar. That's not to say it wasn't beautiful. It WAS! Actually, it was stunning — just not someplace we would have chosen for a spring holiday. It wasn't long before the grass on the slopes was long enough that it needed a bit of trimming. I started to wonder how they went about cutting the grass in the French alps. Dave was impatient to find out; the length of the grass had closed his personal ski slope driving range as he could no longer find his balls! Then one morning I heard a really odd sound in the distance – like a clattering sound, but it also had a kind of ring to it. It was particularly noticeable because it was SO QUIET during lockdown. The noise got closer and closer... until it was overwhelming... and when I next looked out of our balcony window, I could not believe my eyes... COWS!

Cows, Cows, and MORE Cows!

Not just a few, a whole herd! And THEY were here to sort the grass out. Hurray! Dave was excited to soon have his driving range back... But unfortunately, we hadn't thought it all the way through, because of course when cows eat, there's always a by-product. Let's just say that Dave soon realised the long grass was actually a much better alternative than what the ground was now covered with! So the cows brought a rather messy end to Dave's plan to perfect his swing. But it was OK because we were STILL in the French Alps, and actually loving it!

At the time, there was a bit of a sourdough craze happening as people got bored with home cooking and started learning some new skills in the kitchen. So Dave joined in! But he wasn't interested in creating a basic sourdough loaf like everyone else. Instead, Dave decided he wanted to use the opportunity to master the art of making his very own home cooked sourdough Pizzas! So Friday night became pizza night, and week by week we worked out how to make a pretty darn good sourdough pizza with just a frying pan, a hob and a grill.

And of course, what do you do when in France with nothing to do but eat, watch the grass grow, and watch the cows eat the growing grass?

We drank wine.

Lockdown wine bottles, French Alps, spring, 2020

SO. MUCH. WINE!

It wasn't the healthiest we've ever been. Like so many others during lockdown, we enjoyed our share and put on a fair amount of weight along with it. But at least it was some very nice wine, in the French Alps, with a view of... well... mountains and COWS!

Mind you, we had only packed winter gear as we weren't planning to stay into spring. So we had to go clothes shopping, and we really didn't have a lot of options. So, off to Carrefour we went to buy some summer clothes. Carrefour is one of France's big supermarket chains, so definitely more like a big Sainsbury's than a French Connection or something you'd find on Oxford Street in London. We grabbed ourselves some very basic shorts, flip flops, shirts, a baseball cap, etc. Nothing special; only what we needed to avoid walking around in jumpers and jeans.

In June, after two extensions and discussions of a third (!), the French government FINALLY lifted lockdown. Of course, our friends and family had only one question:

Are You Coming Back to the UK?

"Come back to the UK now. It MUST be time!"

But we had other plans...

"Actually, we're doing a road trip."

We stashed our skis in a random ski locker to be collected at the start of the next season. We tossed our winter jumpers in the car. Then, dressed head-to-toe in our highly unfashionable clothes from Carrefour, we hit the road.

Here's me decked out in a pair of their finest shorts and awful flip flops:

Carrefour to the rescue?!

During the break between the first and second lockdowns, we had a great time. We experienced an amazing sense of freedom.

Unexpected Tour

Our road trip took us to the South of France first, and then around the full perimeter of Italy. We spent eight glorious weeks exploring beautiful coasts and vineyards. We stayed in bargain-priced Airbnbs and spent most weekends on the beach. It was a lovely way to recover from being cooped up.

As we started south along Italy's Mediterranean coast in our nice new Audi, quite a few people warned us against driving into Naples. We were told several times, "No, no, no! You can't drive that nice Audi in Naples!" but we were pretty set on our plan to visit the pizza capital of the world and weren't to be swayed. Looking back, I can tell you it was MENTAL! Terrifying. We should have taken their advice, but we managed to survive it, and our new Audi thankfully escaped unscathed.

We also drank a LOT more wine and ate a fair amount of pizza. And finally in September 2020, we made our way home after a full six months away.

Homecoming

By the time we arrived home, I wasn't feeling well. I'd eaten a lot of cheese and cured meats whilst in Italy. I soon found out from my guardian angel Stacey, that if you eat cured meats, and don't also eat anti-parasitic foods like ginger, you can sometimes pick up gut parasites. Well, I'd picked myself up a nasty parasite, and the effect it had on me was terrible...

My regular state is 'Energised... Let's go!' The gut parasite turned that on its head. It was like I became a different version of myself, anxious, teary all the time. I was worried about each day, didn't want to go to meetings, not even wanting to get out of bed in the mornings. I felt totally overwhelmed by the world, had depressive symptoms, and didn't want ANYTHING to do with the business. Looking back it was a pretty scary experience, because I suddenly realised how little control I had over my emotional state. I literally felt like a different person. And had I not had Stacey in my life helping me to understand that these emotional issues were all being caused by the parasite, then I would have thought I was having a mental breakdown!

Thankfully I wasn't, and now in hindsight, I also find it interesting. Before that time — even though we'd been working with Stacey regularly — I had no real awareness of the mind-gut connection. Nobody had ever told me that your gut health can have a profound effect on your mental health. So it was a very powerful way to learn about and experience this connection first hand. This means it is now much easier to notice when mine, or someone else's emotions are being negatively affected by something in the gut.

A Seed of Wisdom Planted

We've made a lot of mistakes, and it always makes me feel better to not only learn from them but pass on that wisdom to others. I'm convinced it would have made a huge difference to us if someone had shared those lessons with us before we did things the hard way.

One of the reasons we came back to the UK was for a 3-day retreat we were running in Margate in September 2020. This retreat was purely for property investors, but totally focused on Business Strategy. It was three days of mapping out a straightforward and actionable plan using the Property Strategy Business Plan we'd developed and refined.

We really enjoyed mentoring people and passing on our knowledge of property. However, the more Dave and I worked with people, the more I started to realise that we were missing a piece of the puzzle. Dave brought amazingly detailed investigative skills and I was great at Strategy. But neither of us was great when it came to mindset and accountability.

I had stayed connected with Dom Beecheno and kept hearing about the incredible work he was doing, guiding successful CEOs, helping them to get clear about what they do and why they do it. And I knew he'd helped hundreds of other business owners. From the time I first worked with him back in 2015, I was impressed with how passionate he was about personal development, mindset, and keeping people accountable.

I also knew that Dom had been an estate agent at one time, so he understood the property market. With that in mind, it seemed natural to ask him to come on board with Property Strategy. By bringing him in, it was like rounding out the circle. So from 2020, Dom has been a key part of Property Strategy to help us support our mentees better. This was the first time we'd run a retreat with him. One night during the retreat, at dinner, I was sitting next to Dom as he was talking to one of the delegates about achieving their goals, when he said:

> *"You see what you have to do is, you have to set yourself a goal, and then... you have to let it go."*

I scoffed! "No way, that is NOT how I made it where I am today!! It has been through HARD WORK, PUSHING, and NOT taking no for an answer...EVER! That's how you make your goals a reality."

Little did I know the true wisdom contained in Dom's words; or that I would be reminded of them more than once in the coming years.

Chapter 14

2020 – The Most Game Changing Year Ever

As we walked to the British Airways check-in desk in Heathrow's Terminal 5 in November 2020, we didn't know if they'd even let us board the flight.

The tension rose as BA staff asked to see our passports. Would they let us through? Did we actually have the authority to leave the country? They asked a few questions, checked our visas and directed us to departures. Next, Dave and I made our way to passport control. Each step along the way we hoped for the best but expected the worst.

Passport control and security both allowed us through. We breathed a joint sigh of relief, but we STILL weren't sure we'd made it. Even if we got on the flight, would South Africa's border control actually let us in?!

Boris Made Us Do It!

It had been a crazy couple of weeks leading up to our mad escape. Remember our skis? We'd left them in a random Airbnb locker in the French Alps. Our plan was to go back at the start of the season and pick them up. Then we'd make our way across the border to Italy where we wanted to spend an entire season skiing. This time (hopefully), without having to watch the snow melt in the spring!

We had every intention of living up to our word to collect our skis. We even set a departure date — the last full weekend of October. It didn't happen. Still suffering from the stomach parasite I'd picked up in Italy over the summer, I wasn't feeling well. So we had put it off by one week.

The weekend we were meant to leave, four ski resorts opened in the Italian Alps. Then, without much fanfare, they all closed again. Apparently, social distancing wasn't being adhered to. Then within a couple of days it was clear that the Alps were NOT going to open again.... AT ALL!!

This was turning into a nightmare. Here in the UK, even though COVID cases had levelled out during the summer, they'd started surging again in the autumn. September had seen the 'rule of six' brought in and a return to work from home[1]. In October, it was the confusing three-tier system with different socialising rules for different areas depending on what tier they fell in.

Then, on 31 October 2020, it happened...

The government announced a 'circuit breaker' lockdown to begin on November 5th. Including a total ban on holidays altogether! We were told that the lockdown would last four weeks to bring COVID transmission numbers down. Here we were, staying in a random Airbnb in the UK, facing ANOTHER lockdown... but this time rather than the adventure of being locked down in a very cool but random location, we'd be stuck in a 1-bed flat in England... during the Winter! This was not what we had in mind.

I looked at Dave and said "Nooooooo! Where in the world can we go? How are we going to get out of the country?! And can we make it out on time before the Government's 'holiday ban' kicks in?!"

Lucky for us, we had an option up our sleeve.

You see, a year prior, we had planned to move to South Africa for 18 months. It was just a life plan thing — something we wanted to do. To move to South Africa, we needed a long-term visa. So we had applied for a

1. The 'rule of six' was a restriction that legally prohibited meeting more than six people socially. It went into effect on 14 September, 2020. (Source: https://commonslibrary.parliament.uk/research-briefings/cbp-9068/)

temporary, four-year 'retirement' visa, which had been granted on the basis that we had enough income coming in from property to qualify. So we were "retiring" to South Africa... in our early 30s!

We'd received our visas in December 2019, just before COVID struck. The plan had been to go to South Africa after our time skiing in the French Alps in 2020. Of course, then lockdown happened, so South Africa didn't happen. The good news was, we still had our retirement visas ready to go.

That week we went through the palaver of all the expensive COVID testing you had to do to be allowed to travel, threw all our stuff in some bags, and made a frantic dash for Heathrow.

Due to how long it took to get the tests booked in and results back, we ended up having to fly one day after the ban on holidays was brought in, which officially meant we shouldn't have been allowed to leave the country. But we'd made our own luck. When we left for South Africa, nobody could stop us because due to our visa, we weren't actually going on holiday. We were emigrating. That was the ONLY reason we were able to get out of the UK just after the second full lockdown came into effect.

Business Class Blues?

Have you ever tried to use air miles on a last-minute booking? Under normal circumstances, it is nearly impossible to get a business class ticket. You have to plan a year in advance as soon as the air miles tickets are released. But during COVID, it was SO EASY!

Despite our last-minute getaway, we managed to get business class flights (they were ALL available!). Even better, Dave had never flown business class before, so he was very excited to get to try out the lounge at Heathrow Airport.

Sadly, as we walked up to the lounge doors, brimming with excitement, our hearts dropped a bit as we saw a signpost sitting directly in front of the doors. Disappointment hit as we realised that there WAS no lounge open at Heathrow, because of COVID. So instead, we wandered the departures lounge looking forlornly for an alternative, and whilst nearly every good food outlet was closed, we eventually found our way to Fortnum & Mason. There, we bought ourselves the most expensive picnic we could imagine to celebrate what had turned out to be a very jammy escape from lockdown in a wintery UK. £100 later, Dave had himself a nice bottle of champagne, and we enjoyed a very lovely (if a bit over-priced) picnic in the departures lounge.

We still use those cool bags that came with the picnic to this day! Maybe it wasn't so overpriced after all.

Cape Town

The border control officer flipped through the pages of our passports.

"What is the nature of your visit to South Africa?"

When we arrived in Cape Town, we weren't 100% sure if we'd be allowed in. They DID let us in, but it was a little tense because even though we had visas, we still hadn't officially 'activated' them yet! So in our minds, there was a tiny chance that border control wouldn't consider them valid.

Once there though, it was amazing. It felt like we were the only tourists in the entire country. At that time, the news coming out of South Africa about COVID was so bad that no one was travelling there, scared for their safety. For us, it was perfect!

Because of the lack of tourists, we were renting incredible villas for next to nothing, at the peak time of the year. We're talking a 5-bed detached house on a golf estate, with its own swimming pool and two built-in barbecues. It was luxury we'd never experienced before. We didn't even consider something unless it was at least 50% reduced from the regular price and had its own swimming pool.

When we left the UK, we'd told family that we would return for Christmas. But with all the talk of "safety bubbles" and another lockdown after Christmas, we were very reluctant to leave the beautiful South African summer. Soon it became clear that the UK lockdowns would be extended beyond Christmas and into 2021.

So, with slightly mixed feelings, we decided it would be best to stay and spend Christmas in Cape Town, and enjoy the luxury we'd unexpectedly found ourselves in. But that isn't all we did...

How We Raised Finance and Did Deals from 'Our' Villas

Whilst the UK was in lockdown and we were in South Africa, we kept doing deals. Our property business was STILL happening without us being there! Over the next six months, we agreed three new deals.

One was 13 flats in Broadstairs— two blocks next to each other:

On that one, we did two deals with different investment partners, splitting the title during purchase so that we could buy both.

The second property was a block of 13 flats in Westgate:

And the third was a block of four flats in Margate:

We sold those four flats off to four different investors as 'sourced deals'. We also agreed another new JV partnership with an awesome family who invested £1 million in our partnership.

We were securing great deals and working with amazing investment partners. The property business was in better shape than we ever imagined it could be – it had surpassed everything we'd ever dreamed of when we started.

My property journey had started with me wanting the freedom to not have to ask to take a holiday. For me, that meant Financial Freedom. Eventually, we realised that the dream life we thought Financial Freedom would bring was actually a fallacy. It was a trap unless you also created Time Freedom. So we expanded our vision to include Time Freedom and worked towards making that happen.

But now we'd achieved another level, a special, unexpected combination of both Financial Freedom and Time Freedom... LOCATION Freedom!

The 24-year-old version of myself was jumping for joy inside... the version of me who'd sat looking out the window in that tiny ski apartment eight years earlier feeling fed up about having to go back to work on Monday... who wanted to be able to go on holidays and travel the world as much as she wanted without having to ask anyone for permission. To have a cashflowing (and growing!) property portfolio! At that moment, that 24-year-old version of myself could not have been happier.

Never in my wildest dreams back in 2013 had I thought it would be THIS GOOD. I never imagined I'd be in some ridiculous, modern villa, overlooking an insane vista of the ocean. Swimming in my stunning PRIVATE swimming pool! Never!

On 25th January 2021, it was my 32nd Birthday. Eight years since the decision to start investing in property. I lay on an inflatable in that infinity pool on a stunning sunny day (with a bottle of alcohol-free beer!) and gazed out at the view. As I let the moment sink in, as I reflected on the highs and the lows, on how far we'd come... I was overwhelmed. But not like the overwhelm I'd experienced before... it was overwhelming gratitude.

This was everything I'd ever dreamed of and so much more. *So this is what it feels like to set a goal and to surpass it... I suppose this is what SUCCESS feels like?* I could not believe Dave and I had done it. Time Freedom, Financial Freedom AND even Location Freedom. This was the freedom I had been searching and dreaming of not just for the last eight years, but for many years before that too.

And as that thought entered my mind, I realised I was overheating in the sun... so I plunged myself into the pool, filled with tingles of joy inside.

Part Two

Chapter 15

Freedom Was Ours... Or Was It?

Around January 2021, everything was about as perfect as it could have been. At that point we were in another incredible 5-bedroom villa, this one with its own 20m infinity pool and a stunning view of the ocean. We basked in sunshine... sitting on our deck chairs ... in South Africa... whilst back in the UK it was grey, rainy, cold and in lockdown.

It was freedom beyond our wildest dreams, and we were still growing our business. With £M's being invested, amazing deals being done, and the team and processes in great shape. We wondered if we should pinch ourselves to make sure it was real.

As we sat there taking in the amazing view, I remember looking at Dave and saying, "Dave, this is beyond ANYTHING I ever imagined we would have."

Dave replied, "Yep, I can't believe this is happening. This is ridiculous."

As I lounged in front of the pool, looking out on the ocean, all I could think was *this is mental!* For a few moments, we just let it sink in. Then — all of a sudden and almost simultaneously — something changed. It was like the energy just shifted.

I said to Dave, "Do you have a kind of background... how do I put it...

nagging anxiety about something? Like something bad is about to happen? Or something is wrong or that somehow this isn't enough?"

Psychological Nudity

Dave said, "Yes, I do have that."

"But there's nothing wrong. No reason for this feeling. This is literally EVERYTHING we've ever asked for and more. So, what is that feeling about?"

Previously, any anxiety or feeling bad like that was tied to something external. Maybe a deal fell through, or a refurb went over budget, or it'd been down-valued. When those feelings came up, I'd think *I need to make sure next time the refurb doesn't go over budget, then I will feel good. Or once this refinance is completed, I'll be able to chill out again and stop feeling worried.*

But right now everything was going to plan! Actually even better than the plan. Everything was as good as it gets. We were on top of the world. What, then, was that feeling?

We'd experienced a lot over the years, but this was different. It wasn't frustration. There was no shame about a project. It wasn't the anger that rises up when a bank reneges on verbal promises. It was the first time we were ever aware of an almost visceral sensation without having something to attach it to.

It was as if by stripping away all the normal business stresses and achieving our primary goals of time, location and financial freedom, we had brought this underlying tension into plain sight. Whilst our conscious, logical minds had been saying *this is awesome*, deep-seated anxiety somehow still had us in its grasp.

Is This How Awesome Feels?

Imagine having worked SO hard, for SO long, to FINALLY be able to say "I'm FREE". This was SUPPOSED to be the dream, the lifestyle that we had been lusting after. Why did we not just feel awesome and happy!? Something wasn't right.

We've all heard the phrase 'money can't buy you happiness'. And we've all heard stories about footballers, entertainers, lottery winners, and even people whose wealth comes from inheritance, who are miserable. But for us it wasn't so much about money. Yes, we'd wanted financial freedom, but our goals had evolved to include time and location freedom. And we'd earned it!

Now that we had it, now that we were 'free', shouldn't we *feel* free?

There's an amazing book called *The Top Five Regrets of the Dying: A Life Transformed by the Dearly Departing*. The author, palliative care nurse Bronnie Ware, asked her patients what they regretted. She wanted to know what they would change in their lives if they could go back and do it all over again. I won't spoil it here — it is worth a read — but I will tell you that #5 on the list was: I wish I had let myself be happier[1].

While it might not be as simple as 'letting yourself be happier' there is a profound truth in the idea of just letting yourself be.

A New Mission

That day, sitting by the pool, something changed. It was a launch pad into a whole new world of exploration about what freedom means. We had everything we thought freedom was... but somehow, crazily... we still DIDN'T FEEL FREE. So we knew we had to start exploring our feelings more deeply and doing some self-reflection. We knew that there was more to all of this, and that we HAD to figure it out. Now that we had achieved the external trappings of freedom, we had a new goal and focus: How can I actually FEEL FREE?

It became our new mission — a mission we continue to this day. It is ALSO our mission to give back and to share our experience with those we mentor.

By that time we'd been mentoring clients for years. Dave and I had a very logical, detailed, strategic process to everything. But we were coming up

1. Bronnie Ware, (2012) *The Top Five Regrets of the Dying: A Life Transformed by the Dearly Departing* (London: Hay House), 157

against some blockages with clients. My 'bash the wall down' approach wasn't working. That was how our business partner Dom came more into the picture. We'd asked him to work with some of our clients who were getting in their own way. Little did I know how much Dom would help me and Dave in the process, too.

Freedom Formula:
The Three Freedoms and You

When we realised something was wrong — as if something was missing — we started a journey of self-reflection and self-exploration to identify what it was. We later came to call this missing aspect 'Emotional Freedom' and it is an essential part of what we now believe in and teach

After we started doing the work and added EMOTIONAL freedom as a goal, we realised that true freedom will NEVER come only from money. Nor will it come from having all the time in the world. To be truly free, you must actually FEEL free.

But to FEEL free requires all three freedoms:

Financial Freedom, Time Freedom, AND Emotional Freedom. It's integral to get all three of these elements of freedom coming together if you want to create YOUR ideal lifestyle. The three BIG freedoms sit at the centre — the core — of our Freedom Formula:

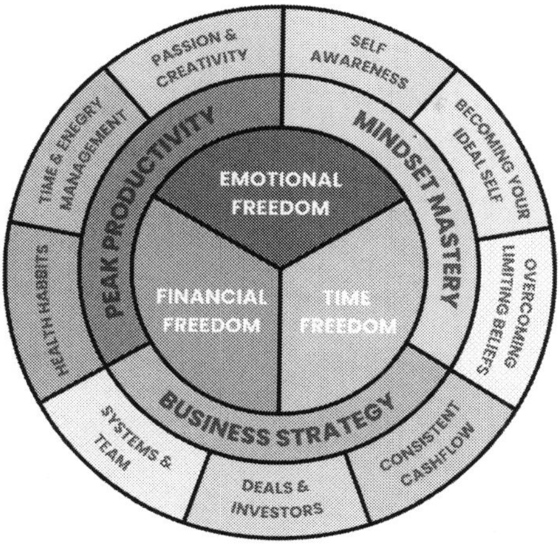

Three Freedoms at the core of our Freedom Formula

How do you achieve this balance? It is easy to look at a diagram and think *Aha! Now I get it. I have to balance financial freedom with time and emotional freedom.* But how, really, does one get there?

The stories in the following chapters will show that even though we thought we had achieved freedom, in the only way that really matters, we hadn't yet. My hope is that as you read you can begin to understand, and embrace, TRUE freedom. YOUR freedom. And to being able to always FOCUS on it above everything else.

Chapter 16

The Positive Spiral

Discovering what true freedom IS didn't happen in a flash of insight. It wasn't an epiphany, where suddenly everything made sense. In that moment, we had more questions than answers. To find the answers, we had to take a new path of exploration.

That is exactly what we did. When we set the new goal to 'feel free' we started working on ourselves. It wasn't a sense of something is wrong with me. It was more like *what is this I'm feeling? What does it mean? How can I change it?*

At this point we were quite anti personal development. We were of the opinion that we didn't need any of that 'woo woo' stuff to achieve what we wanted.

Over the years of knowing Dom, he had suggested various personal development books to me, which I wouldn't prioritise reading. That was until the Autumn of 2020 when I got the parasite and lost control of my emotions for about six weeks — I had been quite desperate for any help that I could get to feel better. At that time Dom suggested I read *A New Earth* by Eckart Tolle – it was the first time I'd opened my mind to something like that. The book was such a completely different way of looking at the world that it kind of blew my mind. I'd encouraged Dave to read it too — but he'd not been interested in it.

Now that I was acknowledging there was something I'd clearly missed in this whole big Freedom search, I started to reflect further on that book and what Dom had said to me: 'set a goal and then let it go'. I'd had SUCH a visceral negative reaction to it just a few months before. But I decided to will myself to open my mind to the fact that maybe, just MAYBE, he might be right.

So from that moment on, any time Dom suggested a book to me I decided I would read it. And more than that, I'd actively go and search out these kinds of personal development books myself too. So I went back to the Dom book suggestion list and downloaded a few books... and I set about avidly reading them every morning.

Meditations

Using meditation as a tool was one of the first big changes I made. Our first business coach, Elliot[1], was into meditation. At the time, I thought *that's so woo-woo. I'll never need that. I'll just hit my to-do list and manage my time.*

There in Cape Town, South Africa, with everything stripped away and time on our hands? We were ready. One of the books we ordered was *Total Meditation* by Deepak Chopra. (When the student is ready, the book will appear?!)

Here's Dave reading it — at our villa with the infinity pool where we had our first realisation — right near the beginning of our self-exploration journey.

1. See Chapter 4: How Holiday Every Six Weeks Was Born

Dave reading Total Meditation *by Deepak Chopra*

One thing about meditation is that you can read about it all you want, but the only way to get anything out of it is to DO IT. I started creating time each day to meditate. Since we were in South Africa (a couple hours ahead of UK time) that space opened up in the mornings.

That's how both Dave and I started sitting in meditation, just exploring, trying to learn to pay attention to our thought patterns, our 'grooves', our desires, and our emotional habits.

On Being Your Own Therapist

Previously, I'd seen a therapist to try and overcome some of my negative thought patterns and self-sabotaging personality traits such as perfectionism. I would go to a therapy session and discuss things with them, and they would help me get clarity or gain insights. I found it really useful but meditation brought this to a new level.

Total Meditation includes a course called *7-Day Meditation Course: Insights for Life.* We found it a great way to start and develop a daily meditation practice. It teaches you to calm your mind and focus on your breath. Then you ask yourself for insights.

I would find a quiet place and go through this *Insights for Life* method each morning. Out of this I started getting awareness that I thought I'd never have — insights I used to see a therapist for. It was a kind of evolution to becoming my own therapist.

Alcohol and The 5 AM Club

It was during this time that South Africa banned alcohol because of COVID. We had an enforced break from alcohol for about four weeks and it was so good that I continued for a further eight weeks. It took a couple of weeks to feel the effects, but suddenly we noticed how energized we were and how easy it was to wake up! That started a positive spiral of getting up earlier. We began getting up with the sun — something I had never been bothered to do before. This, in turn, gave us more time in the morning to read a book in bed with a cup of tea, which is where we found the time to start reading Dom's book suggestions.

As we had more time and felt more energised, we found it easier to start eating healthier. We stopped craving the sweet and fatty foods that we normally ate for an energy boost during the day. Then, because of all that energy, it was easier to exercise more. I must admit, having my own private swimming pool helped!

We had always disparaged the idea of "The 5 AM Club" — this idea that you have to get up early every day to get things done or be successful. But by cutting out alcohol I was suddenly enjoying early mornings and it wasn't an effort to rise with the sun.

Ultimately, it gave me — both of us, actually — more time to work on ourselves. It helped us find an awareness of ourselves that we hadn't had before. We started to uncover how various things in our lives made us feel.

Freedom Formula:
Personal Development Isn't About the Woo Woo

When Dave and I started in property, we didn't bother to do any personal development. We achieved "success" — beyond our wildest dreams — within just eight years without anything in our business being about personal development.

However, I now believe that had we figured this part out — and actually started working on ourselves — we could have cut the time in half. What took us eight years could have been done in four.

You may think like I did: *This personal development stuff is WAY too woo-woo!* (Anti personal development, even!?) Or you might be someone who has always enjoyed working on yourself. Maybe you've dabbled but never really taken it seriously. Regardless, I'd like to share something Dom said to me once:

> "A lot of people get into property because they think there's passive income to be made. They don't realise that, actually, it's a vehicle for your self-development just like any other career... to find out who you really are, what you're best at and how you can use this to serve others."

Read that again.

Keep this idea in mind as you read the rest of this book. Its truth is wrapped up in my story and in Dave's story and in our property investment business. Yes, you will get more ideas you can apply to property. But I hope you take away the idea that any career, business, job — whatever you do, really — is an opportunity to work on yourself.

Again, I was so NOT into personal development. I just wanted financial freedom. And then time freedom. And I was a perfectionist (more on that later, too) who pushed and pushed and GOT THINGS DONE.

When we finally started working on ourselves, it opened a new world. It was liberating. I can't wait to share the rest of our journey with you. If, by reading this book, you've experienced self-reflective moments or questioned your goals, then you are already engaged in personal development... and I promise you, we're just getting started.

Chapter 17

A Beast Rises to the Surface

May 2021 — Camps Bay, Cape Town

The only thing Dave had to do that day for the business was print and sign a mortgage offer, and get it posted back to the UK. It had been arranged for DHL to collect it and the courier was due to arrive in an hour. Simple. Set up the mini-printer, print the mortgage offer, sign, and hand it off to DHL.

Instead, Dave broke down in tears. This tiny job had become too much.

What the F— is going on with Dave? I tried to help him but nothing worked. He was having a breakdown, and I didn't know what to do. It was really hard for me to watch. Dave was the strong one. If I had a bad day, he picked me up. If I was struggling, he would help me. Suddenly, he wasn't able to do that. It was scary.

Officially we weren't even working, we were on holiday, so stress levels should have been low! We were living in an amazing Airbnb villa, but we were still keeping to our *holiday every six weeks* lifestyle. We'd just completed on a deal and had a week off from the business. And it was a great holiday... at least for the first four days.

We'd had an amazing weekend staying at an awesome hotel. We'd been on a helicopter ride around Table Mountain and tried paragliding for the first time. It felt like we were on top of the world. What could POSSIBLY bring you down when you are flying this high?

What Dave didn't know at the time was that something was lurking in the background.

Flying Too Close to the Sun

We'd been working on ourselves, exploring meditation, trying to pinpoint that unease we'd felt in January. Thanks to South Africa's ban on alcohol sales, we weren't drinking much. But we'd also been working on the business, pushing through the purchase of a property in Westgate-on-Sea that had brought a lot of issues with it.

Even though we'd realised something was wrong in January, it still wasn't clear exactly what it was. Dave thought that what he was feeling was just his own form of inner motivation — the drive and diligence required to 'take responsibility for his life' and 'get stuff done'.

In reality, even with all the positive changes he was making, continual stress was really beginning to affect him in a very bad way.

Breakdown

Later, Dave described it as a feeling of complete overwhelm (I can relate to that!). It had been brewing... and this was the moment of breaking.

"All I had to do was print a document and give it to a man from DHL. I literally was having a breakdown about it. A proper, full-on breakdown."

We were living in what looked like heaven, but he felt terrible. That nagging anxiety that we'd both felt was sitting with him all the time.

He kept trying to tell himself nothing was wrong, whilst feeling there WAS something wrong. He kept telling himself he was in heaven, but it felt more like hell. He kept saying to himself *'we're on top of the world'* but the weight of the world was still on his shoulders. It was an ongoing internal conversation he was having with himself.

And that moment — when all he had to do was print a mortgage offer —

the stress and anxiety was suddenly in stark relief and finally took control. This was the true definition of burning out!

KILOS of Epsoms Salts?!

Feeling totally lost about how to help Dave, I remembered advice that Stacey had given me. She'd said that Epsom salt baths are amazing for calming the nervous system down when overwhelmed (I'd had loads of them when I was struggling with the parasite). So I got straight onto it! Always glad to be able to DO something, to be able to help. I ran Dave a bath with several KILOS of Epsom salts and practically forced him to sit in it for half an hour, with tears in his eyes. It was really breaking my heart to see him like this.

Depletion

The bath helped a bit, bringing a functioning Dave back, but the relief was short-lived. Before I knew it, he was crumpled up on the sofa again looking lost and teary eyed. I was desperate to help him, but I just didn't know how! In the end I accepted I couldn't do this alone – I needed help. So I reached out to our Chiropractor:

Stacey, please help me, something has happened to Dave. He's having a breakdown. I don't know why, as we're not experiencing much stress. We're on holiday. I don't know what to do!

Stacey was amazing. Normally, she doesn't do sessions over Zoom. That's because in addition to being a highly trained and experienced chiropractor, she has an in-depth knowledge of holistic health techniques. For example, she is certified in Applied Kinesiology (AK). She understands the physiology of stress and its wide-ranging effects on the body's various systems SO well! But you really need to be in the room for her to figure out the best and most appropriate way to help.

Thankfully, Stacey said she'd see what she could do over Zoom. It was like I was her assistant; she was having me do various tests and telling me to shine a light in Dave's eyes while she monitored his responses.

Finally, Stacey said, "Have you got any of those stomach acid pills that you were taking before with you? Because I think that's what the problem is."

To put things in context, a few years prior to Dave's breakdown, he'd had issues with low stomach acid that had been caused by stress. At that time, Stacey had recommended Betaine Hydrochloride (Betaine HCL) pills and they had worked wonders.

It turns out that the 'background anxiety' (that insidious, low-lying stress that you wouldn't even recognise as stress) had depleted Dave's stomach acid. Again! But MUCH worse this time. It had a cascade effect on his entire body's ability to function. Essentially, it caused a massive burnout — both physically and emotionally.

In case you are unfamiliar, Betaine HCL is a stomach acid 'booster'. It's like a self-diagnosis prescription. To determine how many to take, you start with one pill taken with a meal. If that feels fine, then you take two pills the next meal. Every meal you increase the count until you reach the point where you start to feel a slight heat rising up from your stomach — almost towards acid reflux. As soon as you start to feel anything like that, you drop back a pill. It's a very simple process which you continue until even one pill causes the feeling, and then you can stop. (Please note, this is not medical advice, but an experience share. Consult an expert if you think you may have a similar issue.)

When Dave had experienced low stomach acid before, he'd got up to seven pills per meal. At the time, Stacey said "Wow. That is a LOT."

This time, it was WAY worse!

First, imagine someone who is not good at taking pills. That's Dave... and it is PAINFUL to watch! Like watching a baby bird try to eat a big chunk of bread!

We did happen to have some with us, so Dave started taking them the next day. One pill, two pills, three pills. The next day it was four pills, five pills, six pills. On day three he took seven pills with breakfast... eight pills with lunch... nine pills with dinner...

The Magic Number 14

On day five, when Dave took his 15th pill with dinner, he FINALLY had that slight feeling of warmth. So, he backed off and stayed at 14 pills. Every. Single. Meal. That's how low his stomach acid had become!

Thankfully, Dave had already started to feel better by the third day. Even though he hadn't reached his 14-pill limit, they were starting to work, and he was back functioning at around 50%. As his body responded, the difference was obvious. Dave stayed on 14 pills per meal for the next three months! Can you imagine? We were driving around South Africa to all the health shops trying to find these pills.

"Do you have Betaine Hydrochloride?"

"Yes, just over here."

They'd try to hand me one container of them, and I'd politely ask them to move aside whilst I swept the whole shelf worth into a basket! We would take everything they had because you only get 60 pills in a bottle and Dave was taking 42 every day! He ended up taking Betaine HCL pills for the next 18 months before finally coming off them.

Solutions

Dave's breakdown brought a moment of clarity that something was wrong and whatever it was, it was unsustainable. His mind was telling him he had an amazing life, but his body was telling him a completely different story.

Something Stacey said sent Dave down a whole path of deeper exploration:

"We could solve the stomach acid problem, but SOMETHING is causing it. THAT is what you need to solve, otherwise this will just keep coming back."

She helped us see that Dave's low stomach acid wasn't the actual problem, it was just the symptom. Dave started working on a solution. He'd already been dabbling in meditation since our conversation by the pool in January. Now he started voraciously reading new books, everything he could get his hands on about how to approach life.

Around Christmas of 2021, Dom gave him a copy of *Becoming Supernatural*[1] by Dr. Joe Dispenza. He was reading books on Taosim, yoga, Buddhism, self-help, hypnosis, and on the list goes. One particular book, *Depressive Illness: The Curse of the Strong* by Dr. Tim Cantophor, was extremely relevant. It is about people who are really strong or stoic (just like Dave), who can deal with a lot. It explains how this personality type can only cope up to a certain point before they suddenly break – which is usually a surprise for everyone who knows them. It then goes through the full medical and physiological reason for this breakdown. This brought home the fact that the depressive breakdown Dave experienced was not a psychological affliction, but rather a physiological one.

All the while Dave was trying new things, really digging deep to get to the root cause of the problem. What he learned, not just intellectually but from experience and deep understanding, is that it was all about stress. Stress has the power to affect your body in so many different ways, including lowering your stomach acid. This, in turn, causes the body's hormones and other chemicals to become imbalanced. Ultimately, this can lead to a whole host of physical, emotional and mental maladies. In Dave's case, it expressed as depression.

Freedom Formula: Find the Cause and Solve THAT

In the UK, we have an amazing system where everyone has access to health care. We also seem to live in a time where it is more fashionable to treat symptoms than to look for the actual cause — especially in problems related to stress.

I am not a doctor. I don't have diplomas or certificates on my wall as proof of authority on physical or mental health. And yet, I have witnessed — and experienced first hand — the destructive consequences of long-term, chronic stress.

1. Dave says this book was life changing. It is about neurology and how the body works in relation to your thoughts and emotions, i.e., how they interact from a scientific point of view.

I've also watched (and experienced) the incredible physical and emotional transformation that happens when you take care of the stress rather than just treating the seemingly random symptoms.

The takeaway: Learn to recognise classic stress related symptoms. But also go further and consider learning more about the Mind-Body connection. This is nothing new — the ancient yogis (and others) were talking about it hundreds, if not thousands of years ago. But now there is an increasing amount of scientific data backing up this connection. In the case of your health, knowledge is power, and knowledge is Freedom.

Chapter 18

Conditional Happiness

Dave's breakdown made him realise that he needed to address the root cause of that nagging feeling lurking in the background. It started him on a path of self-exploration, which pulled back the curtains on chronic stress.

Stress manifested itself in a very different way for me and Dave. Whereas Dave let it simmer, I tended to build up to burnout faster. He's much more solid and consistent. For him, stress was a low-lying background issue. He dealt with it for a long time before the little signs started coming. Then he ignored the signs until his body was SCREAMING.

I've always been full of energy; push through and get stuff done. Eventually, I'd burn out and have a small 'breakdown', ending up in tears, as you know from the stories in this book! Mine happened more often, but they were less intense — almost like a release valve. That said, Dave's experience had a PROFOUND effect on me.

My Rock

Between the two of us, Dave had always been the rock. To see him like this shook me. Not just because I care about him. It also made me realise that I had made my happiness conditional on his happiness. Subconsciously, I thought that if he wasn't pleased and happy, then I somehow didn't deserve to be pleased and happy. But suddenly, life presented this opportunity for me to realise that is not the case.

At first, it didn't FEEL like an opportunity! It felt SO out of control. My happiness had been dependent on Dave's happiness, and I couldn't control how he felt. His breakdown meant I couldn't control how he was reacting and feeling. And Dave couldn't help me with how I was feeling. It was like a rug was pulled out from under me.

Stepping Up

That pushed me to step up and take much more responsibility for my own emotional state. I needed to find a way for my emotions to be less affected by Dave, so I looked at how I was (or wasn't) taking responsibility for my own emotions. I started to realise there was a 'people pleasing' part of me. And it was sabotaging SO MUCH of my life and my relationships.

Deep down, I felt like I had to take responsibility for the people in my life. If they were not happy, or healthy, or they were having their own challenges, I took those challenges upon myself to solve for them. This was all going on subconsciously, mind you. It took time and a lot of self-reflection to become aware of it.

But whereas before when I was down I would lean on Dave, I now stopped doing that. Instead, when I started to feel low, I would find a quiet place and meditate. This led to a more consistent and deeper meditation practice — and it was a very important next step in the journey.

Sitting

I would sit each day and bring my awareness to the uncomfortable feeling 'of the day', which, I was surprised to find, was always there in some form or another. Rooted in stress, nagging anxiety, and negative thought patterns, it manifested itself in physical discomfort.

It would usually be some kind of tightness in my lower back, which linked to a sinking feeling in my stomach, and a tension around my heart and shoulders. I started to realise that this feeling was always there at a very low level!

As I became more aware of that 'always on' feeling, I was able to accept it. I started to learn how to stop pushing emotional discomfort away. Instead, I began to allow myself to feel it, to trust that it wouldn't swallow me whole, and that I'd come out the other side again.

Pushing and Pulling

There's an old corporate leadership training exercise about pushing and pulling. Briefly, it works like this:

Two people stand facing each other with palms together. One has been told to push against the other to try to move (manage) them in the direction they want them to go. The other person's instinctual response is to push back. So, the two stand there pushing against each other.

Next, the facilitator whispers into the ear of the 'pusher' and says "Now, gently take them by the hand and, instead of pushing, lead them where you want them to go."

If you've ever done this exercise, you know how the energy completely shifts. People who were getting 'pushed' are quite easily led and 'pushers' turn into leaders instead of managers.

It might sound a little cliché but dealing with uncomfortable emotions can be like this. My instinct, my natural way of dealing with emotional discomfort, was to push it down, to bury it. Whilst that may work for a while, at some point all those negative emotions push back. This can create health issues, or even force a breakdown, which can lead to quitting or giving up. To overcome burying emotions like this, you have to be willing to stop trying so hard to be in control — something that was very alien to me.

Awareness

Meditation helped me to uncover amazing insights about myself that I had been completely unaware of. In doing so, I realised that the world was not to blame for everything I was feeling and I found a way to take responsibility for my own emotions.

The truth is, your reaction is yours. In relation to property investing, I started to realise that with all the challenging things along the way, the negativity I felt was just MY reaction. 'Bad' stuff happens and you react to it. You get downvals, you get a builder who messes up, you make bad hires... but it is YOUR reaction that makes it a negative experience.

Psychologists refer to this as one of the root causes of neurotic conditions[1]. It is the difference between negative experiences and negative reactions. In simple terms, there are three ingredients:

1. **Temperament.** How strongly you react to a negative event. For example, the natural feelings you get when faced with a downval.
2. **Experience.** Real-world problems such as getting screwed over by a builder or hiring the wrong team member.
3. **Reaction to feelings.** How you react to the natural feelings that occur when faced with a negative experience. Do you have negative *reactions* to the negative feelings? If so, and if it becomes habitual, it turns into a vicious cycle that can lead to neurotic disorders, including anxiety and depression.

Like many people, I was not even aware of the third ingredient above. I had always thought that when bad things happen, I must control those factors in the future. It was up to me to make sure they didn't happen again. As long as I was in control, I'd be happier.

Through meditation, I started to understand what I could, and could not, control. I started thinking *actually, you know what? I can't control any of this. All I can do is show up, do my best, take responsibility for how I feel, and the rest will happen how it happens.*

On a more personal level, what Dave was going through pushed up against my deepest fears. As I continued to meditate, deep-seated thoughts surfaced. I realised I was harbouring irrational fears:

---

1. Psychology Today (2018) *It's Not the Negativity but Your Reaction to It* - Available at: https://www.psychologytoday.com/gb/blog/theory-knowledge/201801/its-not-the-negativity-your-reaction-it (Accessed: 8 May 2024).

- I felt I did not deserve to be happy if those around me were not happy.
- I feared that if those around me were unhappy, that they would leave me.
- And... I'd be left totally abandoned and alone with no family or friends.

Yikes!! Of course, this train of thought was irrational, but on a subconscious level that's what I felt. I realised I had to start to let go of these subconscious fears so that I could find my happiness regardless of what was going on with Dave (or anyone else in my life for that matter). And, as a result, I could be there for Dave in a much more unconditional loving way.

Real Versus Imagined

From all our avid reading, research, and personal experiences, we started to learn a lot more about fear, and the power of it. Fear is a natural protective mechanism that is coded-in to our DNA. It is there to let you know when you are in danger. The problem, as it turns out, is that our brains don't know the difference between real and imagined experiences. In fact, the brain and body respond almost exactly the same way to your imagination as they do to the reality around you.

Let me just re-iterate that... **the brain and body respond almost exactly the same way to your imagination as they do to the reality around you.**

This blew me away when I started reading about it. It turns out this has been scientifically proven in hundreds of different experiments, all designed to find out how much impact the mind and our imagination can have on the body. It's an incredibly powerful realisation that has transformed how we respect the things we fill our mind with. So let me share them with you here too... The following experiment[2] was featured in the May edition of the 1992 Journal of Neurophysiology.

---

2. Yue, G. and Cole, K.J. "Strength increases from the motor program: comparison of training with maximal voluntary and imagined muscle contractions", *Journal of Neurophysiology*, (May 1992) Available at: https://doi.org/10.1152/jn.1992.67.5.1114

In this experiment, the scientists wanted to determine whether practising the piano with your mind could affect your finger strength as much as practising it physically. As such, they designed an experiment with three groups:

- Group 1: Participants were given a simple physical exercise to practise, five times a week for four weeks.
- Group 2: Participants were shown the same exercise but were told to only imagine practising it for four weeks
- Group 3: Was the control group. Participants were shown the exercise but not required to practise either physically or with their imagination.

At the end of the four weeks the objective method of assessing the results was by measuring the finger strength of the candidates, and the results were as follows:

- Group 1 saw an **increase in finger strength of 30%** from their physical practice.
- Group 2 saw an **increase in finger strength of 22%** from their imaginary practice.
- Group 3 saw no increase in finger strength.

That's right, a 22% INCREASE in muscle strength, just from IMAGINING doing something! The body literally thought it was doing it and responded with a physical change.

I also read about a very similar experiment that was carried out with bicep curls, and the results were the same. Those who did bicep curls every day saw the largest increase in muscle mass. Those who did nothing saw no increase in muscle mass. And those who just imagined doing bicep curls saw an astounding 20% increase in muscle mass in their biceps!

This concept seems crazy, and the ramifications for us are huge. Our minds are constantly creating physical responses in the body just based on what's going on in our minds. That includes responses to our fears. So if you are holding irrational fears, whether conscious or unconscious, they are affecting you — most likely in ways that you aren't even aware of.

This issue is the very foundation for all our subconscious self-sabotage and is something that we are all affected by. It's much easier to see it in others than in ourselves, because it's so difficult to have a clear perspective when looking at yourself. This is why so many of us believe we don't self-sabotage. I was definitely one of those people, but now I can see just how wrong I was.

Understanding the power of my mind has made me become so much more careful with what I fill my thoughts with, because I can now see that what I think about gets strengthened. So I can either focus on strengthening my unhelpful fears that hold me back, or I can use my mind to practice and imagine a new version of myself.

Nowadays, identifying and working to let go of my subconscious fears has become one of the most powerful personal development tools in my arsenal. I've found that doing this regularly helps me to see the drivers for my decisions with far more clarity. It stops my business from getting stuck due to decisions coming from the motivators like irrational fear.

Freedom Formula:
The Art of Letting Go of Irrational Fears

In the next chapter we'll explore the relationship between physiology and emotions (and how it affects your property business). If you struggle with irrational fears, try the following:

5 Tips to Start Letting Go of Irrational Fears

1. **Meditate.** By now, you know I can't recommend meditation highly enough. There is SO MUCH research backing it as a way to deal with stress. But it went even deeper for me. It uncovered my subconscious irrational fears AND helped me begin to overcome them.
2. **Own what you CAN control.** What parts can you control? What are you willing to change? What actions are you willing to take? By looking at the actions and results that are within your control, it also brings clarity to those parts that are not in your

control. Then by focusing your plans and actions on the things within your control, it becomes easier to let go of the other areas, accepting that nothing you do will make a difference to them, and that's fine.

3. **Pause and breathe.** This sounds so simple, and it is. It also works as a way to change your state. Assuming you've identified an irrational fear, you may start to notice the related emotions rising up and your mind becoming distracted. Focus on your breath. Don't allow your mind to follow the thoughts that come up. Instead, pay attention to how your breath feels moving into and out of your lungs. Be aware of the expansion and contraction of your ribcage. Notice if your breath is smooth or 'ragged'. Notice how your breath sounds. Only breathe deep. Breathe slow. Breathe. This does two things: Firstly, it gives your vagus nerve the signal to activate your parasympathetic nervous system[3]. This will move your body's response system out of fight or flight mode and back into rest and relax mode. Secondly, it gives your mind something to focus on other than whatever is causing fear. This stops you from getting drawn into the downward spiral of fear-based thoughts, which is the opposite of what we're trying to achieve. It then allows you to move past the body's fear response so that you can look at the cause of the fear with much more perspective and clarity.
4. **Explore relaxation techniques.** There are so many different ways to get the mind and body into a relaxed state. Find one that works for you consistently. Then use it as your go to technique for processing and letting go of fears. Here are two simple ideas: 15 minutes of yoga or a 15-minute walk/run.
5. **Face your fears.** For me, this started to happen when I realised I could feel things whilst in meditation and come out the other side.

---

3. The sympathetic nervous system is responsible for the 'fight-or-flight' response. It prepares the body for strenuous physical activity and controls our reaction to stress. In contrast, the parasympathetic nervous system works to promote maintenance of the body while at rest. It controls basic bodily functions. sometimes referred to as 'rest-and-digest'. For a deeper understanding of the autonomic nervous system, I recommend *Heal Your Nervous System: The Five Stage Plan to Reverse Nervous System Dysregulation*, by Dr. Linnea Passaler (2024) Fair Winds Press, Beverly, MA, USA.

I found that once I became aware of the fear lurking in my subconscious, I could look straight at it. Then I could see it for the irrational thought pattern that it was and rob it of its power over me. If the fear starts to rise again then I use the breathing method above to regain my perspective. For some people, e.g., those with serious phobias, this method is often done in the form of cognitive behavioural therapy (CBT) or exposure therapy[4].

4. Note: I am not trained in psychotherapy or psychiatry. I am merely passing on information based on my experience and exploration.

Chapter 19

The Swirling Vortex of Chaos (Chemicals, Thoughts, Emotions)

The growing awareness we had of ourselves, thanks to our new morning routine, gave us huge insights. Informed by all the amazing books we were reading, it helped to show us clearly how physiology affects emotions. But even with time working at it, we weren't expecting ANYTHING like a stress-induced depressive breakdown. With Dave's breakdown, we could see — first-hand and with stark clarity — how chemical imbalance affects emotions, which then impacts your thoughts.

Always Stressed? You Might Be an Addict

As we tried to understand what was going on with Dave, we found ourselves deep in understanding physiology. We discovered that every time you have an emotion the body releases hormones. For example, when we are stressed the adrenal glands release adrenaline and cortisol. These chemicals cause a physiological reaction in the body which is supposed to help you deal with the external situation you are facing. This is what we then 'feel' inside.

In the case of cortisol and adrenaline, the body's reaction stems from our caveman roots. Stress was a response to life threatening situations, such as a sabre-toothed tiger bearing down on us. Because of this, these two chemicals cause several reactions to help us fight or run from that threat, including:

- Greater ability to focus by removing our peripheral awareness (tunnel vision).
- Increased heart rate so that more oxygen is pumped around the body.
- More blood and oxygen sent to our muscles to increase their ability to perform.
- More blood sent to the brain to make us more alert.
- Raised blood sugar levels for more energy.
- Reduced inflammation so that the body doesn't experience pain as much.

And the list goes on and on!

The main problem is that what we perceive as a threat in the modern world is mostly not life threatening. Therefore, these physiological responses aren't necessary or helpful to us. And if you continuously face stress, then your body stays in 'threat mode' and keeps releasing small amounts of these chemicals. Eventually the body gets used to them and requires more and more to get the same result (as with any drug).

In the modern world — especially in Western society — we all seem to face a continuous onslaught of non life-threatening stress. So we are getting doses of adrenaline and cortisol on a regular basis and, as that happens, the body **starts to expect** those hits of its favourite drugs. It starts wanting, craving, aching for them. Which means, quite literally, the body gets addicted to them. So, if you find yourself constantly getting stressed, then it's not because the world is stressful, but rather because you have a chemical addiction to your stress hormones.

Imagine, you are having a great time (as we were in South Africa). You're on holiday, doing amazing things, staying in great hotels and epic villas. It's all supposed to be nice and nothing around you should be causing any stress.

Then... the addiction kicks in. The body starts craving the drugs. *Where're my chemicals? Where's my hit? Give me my hit!*

Unlike the drug addict who must go in search of the next hit, your body makes these chemicals all by itself.

So now the mind, on a subconscious level, starts to respond to the body's addiction. It wants to release the chemicals, but the chemicals are only made when feeling anxiety, anger, fear, or other stress emotions.

So, the body asks for the chemicals and begins the emotional cycle by creating a little bit of anxiety purely because it needs its hit. The mind then notices that slight anxiety and, instead of understanding that it's just the addiction, it 'rationalises' the feeling:

Why am I feeling anxious all of a sudden? Oh, yeah, that build is going wrong, it is over budget and the builder's tools got stolen and this could delay the project and...

Then, because the mind is now working on the chosen reason for anxiety, it fires neurons that send a chemical signal back into the body telling it to release more of the desired chemicals:

Oh yes, I should definitely be worried, because this valuation I'm waiting for might come back low... another down val... how am I going to repay my investors if I get down valued? This could ruin my entire business!

Now your mind has found a good reason to be truly worried rather than just a little anxious, and the body responds by releasing even more of the chemicals.

Having this understanding of physiological processes was really helping us to make sense of what Dave was experiencing internally and why he was struggling so much.

The Cycle of Addiction

It turns out that we have this cycle going on inside us all the time. The body and mind are always communicating, and each response intensifies and escalates the reaction in the other. This is what causes those downward emotional spirals we all sometimes experience. And it's why it can be incredibly hard to break out of them.

In the end, what this really means is that we are addicted to being who we are. If you frequently feel slightly anxious, be it from work or life in general, it is your body's subconscious response. It releases the hormones that you are historically most used to. Many people don't even identify it as anxiety. That's because when they have that uncomfortable feeling, it immediately gets covered up. The habitual response makes them feel better. For example, I covered up my own anxiety by being the one who always gets things done:

Push through, bash down walls, let nothing hold you back!

Once I took the time to look beyond my thoughts and actions, I realised this approach to life was a coping mechanism. Whenever I was feeling slightly anxious, pushing through gave me something to do. It enabled me to ignore and overcome the underlying feeling of anxiety.

I am far more conscious of these responses to anxiety nowadays. As soon as I notice the underlying fear driver, I go through the process I shared in the last chapter.[1] But for most people who aren't aware of their habitual responses, the obvious next step is usually to make a big change. They try to remove what they think is causing the anxiety. They change careers or move away from the nasty neighbour. And here's where it gets really interesting. Due to our addiction to these stress chemicals, the body isn't satisfied with this. It doesn't say *Thanks, I was getting a bit fed up with all that cortisol.* Instead, like any drug addict, it will eventually just say *NO! I want my chemicals!*

Then the cycle starts again. The body forces it, the brain responds, something feels wrong, you feel worried about something, the chemical hit comes, and the body says *Excellent, now I'm back to being who I normally am.* This is one of the reasons that it's so hard to change your natural way of reacting to the world, and why personal development can be so hard.

The more I learnt about the body's physiological response, the more captivated I was. Also, kind of annoyed! Why had I never found out about this before? Surely this is something that we should be taught at school. It seemed so fundamental to understand all this to be able to get the most out of life in the modern world.

The Neurological Tramlines

As if being addicted to our own hormones isn't enough, it turns out that there's another issue we have to contend with – our neurological programming.

What we uncovered is that every time we have a thought or take an action, our brain fires off an electrical signal down a neurological pathway. Every different thought or action has its own unique neurological pathway. These electrical signals are the brain's method of both thinking and communicating with the body.

Every time we *repeat* a thought or action, the brain adapts very slightly to make it easier to use that same neurological pathway next time. This is called neuroplasticity and it is one of the most powerful learning tools at our disposal. It is how we learn to do things without consciously thinking about them. When we do something like riding a bike or driving a car for the very first time, it takes a lot of concentration and focus. But as we practise and repeat that action it gets easier, until finally we can do it without any thought at all. It is as if the brain is laying down tramlines to enable quicker and easier movement of electrical currents as they go about their business.

The problem comes when we regularly experience negative emotions or thoughts that create stress. The brain can't distinguish between something we want to learn and something we'd rather not experience again. Every time we experience the same emotion or thought pattern, the brain adapts. It strengthens and streamlines those specific neurological pathways.

This is the foundation of our subconscious programming. It becomes the basis of our personality and belief systems. Over our lives, we continually 'practise' our emotional response to the world by responding to things in a similar way each time they happen. We then rationalise those responses with a thought or belief that 'explains' what we believe has prompted that emotion. Every time we react with that same emotion and subsequent rationalisation it strengthens our programming. Ultimately, we create a new automated response system that saves us from having to consciously think about it in the future.

For example, as a child you may have really desired an ice cream. Every time you had an ice cream, you had a positive emotional response. You might then have thought something like *Wow, Ice cream makes me feel SO GOOD*. Each time you had an ice cream, it got easier for the body to have the positive emotional response and associated thought. Eventually, you didn't even need the ice cream to have the positive feeling. Just seeing an ice cream van would do it. The brain created a neurological pathway linking the desired thing with a feeling of happiness. Your body learned to react with the positive feeling based on thought alone.

At the same time, this experience ingrained a subconscious belief — that you can make life better with sweet foods. This means that every time things get hard or stressful, you reach for the Ben & Jerry's. As an adult, you may not even remember why, but when you hear an ice cream van you immediately feel happy. And no matter how hard you try, you can't help putting on weight when life offers up a stressful situation!

Every time your body gives you that hit of stress hormones, and you think about all the reasons you should be stressed, your brain is busy in the background, hardwiring your thought process and emotional reaction. This is the chemical and neurological patterning that we all contend with. It is always there as a habitual pattern. That's why our personalities get set or stuck — because beneath the surface, we have become like automatons, reacting to the world through habit rather than free will.

I couldn't believe what we were discovering. It was not only helping to make sense of what Dave was going through, but it was also making sense as to why focusing on Financial and Time Freedom wasn't enough. We could NEVER truly be free without mastering our own minds! This is what TRUE freedom was about. It was the ability to CHOOSE to feel free. Emotional Freedom was what we had been missing this whole time.

We were now firmly on our quest to master Emotional Freedom, to figure it out, and be able to bring it back to the property industry. THIS was the missing piece of the puzzle!

Divine Dave

We joke now about how Detail Dave could rebrand as Divine Dave because, through study and meditation, he basically reset his entire system. During the writing of this book, I asked Dave if he had any further insights about this swirling vortex of chemicals, thoughts, and emotions.

He said, "I wish they told me this at school — that you have the power to change your neurological pathways and emotional habits."

Most (if not all) of the people we work with are action oriented. It's not a surprise because that's what we're taught at school. But Western society is inadequate when it comes to understanding holistic health. Yes, in some respect things have changed in the past couple of decades, but this information is still not taught in school. Young people are told that what's important is to work on their physical health, to exercise and get fit, to achieve their ambitions and to make something of themselves in the world.

No one at school says "Let's sit down and meditate. Work on yourself."

But to become who you really want to be requires sitting down to work on what's inside. You CAN change your thought process and your thought patterns. But it's through meditation and not go, go, go…!

Blame Property?

One interesting outcome from Dave's breakdown and subsequent awakening is that he nearly gave up on property. To him, property was the underlying reason, the cause for his background anxiety. So he started to struggle with the property business at this point.

He even went so far as to blame property. In the context of what you've just read about regarding the brain's ability to rationalise, this makes sense. His brain was trying to comprehend the situation and was pinning the stress on his external circumstances. Whilst in reality, it was not property that was to blame, but rather his REACTION to property. So the big question arises, what causes our reactions?

The Illusion

None of this happened in one blinding light of realisation. So if you've started down the meditation path, give it time. Let it unfold.

During the next several months, we started to understand the difference between **what's happening** in the world and **how we felt** about it. It became clear that there need not be a connection and that we can choose to separate the two.

It wasn't long before we realised that everything we thought we knew for certain was an illusion. For example, it's not true that if something like a down valuation happens that you have to feel bad and stressed about it. That's just a subconscious, habitual behaviour pattern learnt from past experience. In fact, the past experiences controlling our reactions are often entirely unrelated to what's happening now!

For example, you may have never even experienced a down val before! So the subconscious works out the correct emotional response based on past experience. You could have a negative reaction based on something that happened on the school playground as a six-year-old. Or it might go back even further...

Your reaction on the playground could have been subconsciously connected to something that happened to you as a baby. This means that your negative reaction to the down valuation was already decided as your brain was still forming!! At that point, you were so young you didn't even have any ability to rationalise or be logical. Everything was instinct based on the fear response system encoded in your DNA as a survival mechanism. That's why the automated response is nearly always a stress response. The body's fear response system evolved to protect us from external threats. At the most basic level, stress is the best way to help our species survive.

It's mad if you think about it. We all believe that our reactions to the world are rational and logical. The truth, as it turns out, is that most of our subconscious behaviour patterns were set by the time we were 10 or 11 years old. Then, over our teenage years we rationalise these automated emotional reactions. This is how our newly formed logical brain attempts to make sense of the world. Then, as adults, we come up with lots of intelligent reasons as to why our reaction is the right one!!

As Dave and I began looking back on our lives, we started to see things with a whole new perspective. With fresh eyes, we came to realise that everything that we thought was bad at the time, had actually turned out to be GOOD! Hindsight is 20/20, right? The only thing that was bad was our perception and the resulting emotional reaction to whatever was happening. We realised that if we could find a way to change our perception in real time, then we could completely change our emotional reactions. In its most optimised version, this would mean no longer seeing anything as negative. We could totally break free of those negative addictions.

Another thing I realised is that we all practise our bad emotional habits by accident. We then justify them either by blaming the world or thinking things like *Well that's just how I'm wired, why should I have to change?*

What we don't do (because we're never taught how) is to proactively practise POSITIVE emotional habits. It seems so obvious to me now! Our brains are always adapting and rewiring based on repetition. So why don't we take the time to wire in things that are helpful to us? So many of us are happy to make time for the gym to change our physical body. So why aren't we willing to find the time to make changes to the structure of our brains? What's even crazier is that we all chase this illusive thing called 'happiness' by struggling for external things like money and wealth. But happiness happens internally. So why don't we focus inwards to find the magical feeling that we all desire? And then there's the catch 22 issue... The fight and struggle for happiness is actually one of the main causes of stress!! In fact for most of us, it is the PRIMARY CAUSE of unhappiness!

Like it or not, stress is affecting your health and business. But I'm here to tell you that you do have the power within to change it. Here's a practical method to help you change the way property (or even LIFE) related stress affects you. We'll use a down valuation as an example.

When something externally triggering happens, the first reaction is always emotional. That is built-in and you can't change it. Emotions are chemical responses, and they happen faster than you can think. For example, imagine you just saw a car crash and someone injured was lying in the road in front of you. Your first reaction would be a visceral emotional response. It might feel like your stomach had jumped upwards into your chest leaving a gaping hole of shock and fear deep in your belly.

You might feel a tight constriction in your heart and throat — a feeling of panic. You would be in shock maybe thinking something incoherent like *Aaaaaaaargh, WTF!!!* Finally, your brain would kick into gear and start thinking something like *Woah how did that happen? I wonder who was at fault? Is that person ok? Should I try and help them, or call an ambulance? Is anyone else injured? Wow! That was really scary! I'm glad it wasn't me!*

Your first response to the world is **always** emotional, and then you start thinking. You try to justify it or understand it logically.

Every time you have an experience and an emotional response followed by thoughts, you create or reinforce a neural pathway. And with each repetition, the neural pathway gets stronger and more difficult to break.

The reality is that these negative emotional responses cause more problems than they solve. In an ideal world, as soon as you had a negative emotional response, you'd be able to say to yourself *I'd rather not have that feeling, thanks very much.* Then you would choose another more positive emotional response instead. Sounds impossible right? Of course, it is not as simple as just saying to yourself *From now on I won't get emotional about a down val.* But I promise you it's most certainly possible to train yourself to do this.

If you want this superpower (because that's what it feels like when you manage it), you have to work on changing how you react.

Freedom Formula:
How to Feel Great About a Down val

This is Dave's method for changing how he reacts, which has been designed from a number of different books he's read. If you want to go deeper on this, then we've found the most powerful book to read is *Breaking the Habit of Being Yourself* by Dr Joe Dispenza. This book scientifically explains everything I've mentioned above (but in more detail) and it all builds towards a comprehensive meditation process designed to rewire your brain's neural pathways for better emotional reactions.

Dave's method takes Dispenza's ideas and then incorporates some more elements from other experts in this area.

Here's the overview:

Phase 1. Practise Positive Responses
To start, you need to spend time practising your ideal responses, your positive emotions.
There is a programme on Netflix called *From Stress to Happiness* which was all about a Buddhist monk called Mattieu Ricard who is known as 'the happiest man in the world'. He has mastered the ability to feel the emotion of happiness whenever he wants to, and his brain waves are off the chart with happiness levels when he meditates. This is the foundational work we need to embark on and gets the positive hardwiring in place for us to have access to when wanted.
Phase 2. Detach from the Negative
Then imagine the exact moment that one of your negative emotional habits would be triggered, and practise detaching from the negative emotion.
Phase 3: Replace the Negative with the Positive
Once you have detached from the negative emotion, you can then practise replacing it with a positive one instead. This imaginary practice rewires your brain, physically changing the old neurological pathways and creating new ones in their place, so that when the triggering event happens in real life, you have laid down the 'tramlines' for your new positive response to happen instead.

These are the steps to take:

1. **Get Calm and Centred.** Before starting any meditation work, it's important to calm your body and mind so that you can remove distraction and focus on the work you are about to do. One of the easiest ways to do this is to focus your attention on your breath for a few minutes. Doing several repetitions of counting to four on the inhalation, holding for four, exhaling for four, then holding for four works really well for me. But there are loads of different breath exercises you can play with.

2. **Practise a Positive Emotion.** Once you are calm, then choose the emotion you want to practise such as Joy, Happiness or Love. Bring to mind an experience in your past when you felt that emotion strongly and relive the memory. Once you've found that emotion, focus on it and allow the memory to slip away while holding the emotion in place. See how long you can keep the emotion going without having to replay the memory.
3. **Imagine a Negative Emotional Situation.** Choose a negative emotional habit you no longer wish to have, such as feeling stressed before a meeting, or receiving a down valuation. Bring to mind the experience that would normally trigger this emotion, and visualise the events and actions leading up to the moment that you felt the emotion.
4. **Detach from the Emotion.** As soon as you start feeling the negative emotion, stop your imagination and focus purely on the emotion. The idea is to interrupt the emotion before it can fully manifest as it normally would, and before your brain has time to start rationalising it. Then consider the emotional reaction from a purely physiological perspective. Where do you feel it in your body? What does it manifest as physically? Is your heart rate higher? Has your temperature changed? Remind yourself that this is purely a chemical reaction inside. The aim is to detach the physical response from the emotions you normally perceive them to represent.
5. **Accept and Let Go.** Accept that these feeling are just your human survival mechanism kicking in and stop fighting them. Accept that they are unrelated to the current experience you are having and are just based on your past experiences. Let go of any thoughts that come up to justify the emotions. Let go of any belief that these emotions are who you are or that you need them. Finally, Let go of the emotion itself (as best you can) saying to yourself that you would rather choose your own response.
6. **Replace with a Better Emotion.** Go back to the moment that you interrupted, your imaginary experience, and think about what the 'awesome' version of you would feel. What positive perspective would that best version of you have? Choose a positive emotion that this 'awesome you' would feel rather than your old

habitual response. Now proactively bring that emotion up (that's why we have to practise them). Bring it into your body and really feel it. Associate the imaginary experience with this new positive emotion. This may take a while to do the first time, but the idea is that you repeat it and practise it in order to 'hard wire' that new emotional response. And each time you practise, it will get quicker and easier. And that's the proof that you are physically creating and strengthening new neural pathways in your brain, just with your imagination.

This is probably a much more 'active' version of meditation than you've come across before. And it is so empowering! You can literally 'rewire' your brain doing this. It takes time and requires thoughtful reflection and practice. But if you do it, you will find your emotional responses in the moment will begin to change. You will find that the initial hit of negative emotion starts to soften, and you'll have more and more control over your thoughts and perspective. You'll no longer be pulled down into a 'this is a disaster' mentality, and instead will move straight to a silver lining and problem-solving mindset. Eventually you'll have hard-wired in the positive response and pruned the negative emotion entirely, giving you full control over your emotions. I assure you, it is worth every minute spent if you want to achieve true freedom.

Chapter 20

You're Doing Deals from Where? (Paradise Island, The Maldives)

"You haven't heard the workaround? All you have to do is go to the Maldives for 10 days, then you can get back into the UK."

By May 2021, we'd been in South Africa for seven months. We had stayed for a month at a time in seven different EPIC villas. It was amazing, but winter was coming to South Africa and we were finally ready to return to the UK. There was only one problem...

It was still the age of Covid-19 and South Africa was on the UK Government's 'red list'.

The red list had started in February. That month, the UK Government announced mandatory quarantine for travellers entering the UK from 33 high-risk ('red list') countries. Travellers from those countries would have to stay in a designated 'quarantine hotel' for 11 nights (at their own expense) before they could move freely about the UK. There was also an amber list which required 10 days of self-isolation.

The list was reviewed by the Government every three weeks and changed regularly. By May there were more than 40 countries on the red list and 170 (most of the rest of the world) on the amber list. South Africa had been on the red list the entire time. It wasn't the best situation for us trying to get back to the UK!

The Government had also published a roadmap for lifting the lockdown. In May, outdoor events and family gatherings were expected to be allowed to go ahead. Our families were planning to get together. We wanted to come back but had ZERO interest in staying in a quarantine hotel.

"Dave, this is the best thing EVER!"

That was when someone we'd met in South Africa told us about the Maldives 'work around'. I couldn't believe it - the Maldives was on the GREEN LIST! What a way to get back to the UK - we just had to be willing to stay there for at least 10 days. Sign me up!

We started planning our trip and the prices were AMAZING! Nobody was travelling to the Maldives due to COVID so there were insanely cheap deals. I was so excited as I'd always wanted to visit the Maldives... 10 days in paradise, here we come. But, as soon as we'd chosen our island paradise and got something booked...

The Maldives went on the red list.

You can't make this stuff up! So, we were back to square one, looking for other ways to get back to the UK without having to stay in a dreaded quarantine hotel. The problem was that the list was always changing. And on top of that, different countries and regions had different rules which were all changing at different times.

As we continued to look, I kept thinking my heart was really set on the Maldives. I want to go to the Maldives.

"Dave?"

"Yes?"

"Did you really want to go to the Maldives?"

"Yes!"

"It feels like the universe is making it very difficult to see your family right now? Maybe we should we just give up on the UK and head to the Maldives anyway?"

Dave looked at me and said "Yeah, f— it. Let's go. We'll go for a month. Maybe it will come off the red list by then. Let's go!"

And, so, we hopped on not one... not two... but THREE planes to get to the Reethi Beach Resort, Fonimagoodhoo Island, the Maldives.

Long On Sun Cream

One thing we did do before we left South Africa was to buy a LOT of sun cream. As you can imagine, it is very expensive in the Maldives because it's a nation of very small islands. So we wanted to make sure we weren't ripped off by the local prices.

Our 'stash' of sun cream we hauled from South Africa to the Maldives

Extended Visa? Yes!

You don't need to apply for a visa before travelling to the Maldives. All you need is a valid passport, proof you plan to leave — such as an outbound flight reservation — and money. You can stay for up to 30 days without having to pay for a visa. However, once we arrived, we discovered that you can extend your visa for an additional 60 days. Let's see...

90 days at Paradise Island whilst the rest of the world worried about COVID? Yes, please!

So, we went for the extended visa.

Doing Deals from Paradise

Whilst in the Maldives, our property business kept growing. We discovered that, yes, you can print personal guarantees (PG's), find a waiter to witness them, and book a DHL delivery even from an island! The only real obstacle was that someone from the hotel had to take the PGs to the main island for us, because that's where the DHL office was.

We had an amazing time in the Maldives. And because we were five hours ahead of the UK, we had so much time in the mornings to ourselves before anyone from the UK was even awake. We were aware of the odd phenomenon that humans tend to fill the time available to them. So during this three months, we used the opportunity to try cutting down the available time and see if we could run our business on fewer hours. To this end, we cut down our working hours to just four hours a day (9:00 a.m. – 1:00 p.m. UK time which was 2:00 p.m. – 6:00 p.m. Maldives time). We then used the extra time in the mornings to work on ourselves instead. It was life changing — an incredible time of personal space and self-reflection. We both evolved a lot during our stay, finding a new balance between our life and our business.

But, it turns out that there is a limit to how long you can spend in paradise! For us, it was about 2.5 months! Because eventually, I started thinking *I'm ready to get off this island.* We also still had to get back to the UK to get our COVID vaccinations, as not being vaccinated was causing a lot of difficulties with our travel plans.

However, before I continue with our travel adventure (you didn't think it was over, did you?) let's take a look at how we made use of three months at Paradise Island. Not the tourist stuff. (Yes, we did that, too! And I literally have the scars to prove it...)

Rather, how we used this time to continue our journey of self-exploration.

Freedom Formula:
The Morning Routine

In South Africa, we had started exploring meditation and reading a variety of books. Now, in this truly beautiful island paradise, with so few people around, we became ultra-focused. Our physical and mental health became our top priority. Whereas before we'd been meditating for 20 minutes each morning, now we developed a whole morning routine.

Our morning routine included:

- A minimum of 30 minutes of meditation.
- Some form of movement or exercise ranging from a short walk to 15 minutes of yoga, or a swim. The key is we made it a habit.
- 45 minutes daily listening to personal development courses. We subscribed to Mindvalley, which has courses on mind, body, soul, relationships... you get the idea. You can listen for 20 minutes a day and, over time, benefit from a variety of experts. Dave found a course by Paul McKenna called *Everyday Bliss, Hypnosis for Instant Freedom from Stress and Anxiety* to be very useful. Mindvalley is a great place to start if you are new to personal development. Or if you feel stuck.
- 45 minutes reading of personal development and/or spiritual books daily.

Resources: Books We Found Useful

By now you've figured out that this is not your typical property investing book. My guess is, you won't find a list of recommended books like the following in any other book on this subject. That's because every other book, training, mentorship program, you name it, is focused on the 'make money' side of property: Financial Freedom. A select few might get to Time Freedom.

To my knowledge, no other property investment mentors are willing to step up and say that Financial Freedom is great, and Time Freedom is amazing, but to be truly free you have to add Emotional Freedom into the equation. It completes the triangle.

With that in mind, the following is a list of books Dave and I have found useful in our quest for Emotional Freedom. The books are listed in no particular order and a few of them have been mentioned in previous chapters:

Recommended Reading on Your Path to Emotional Freedom

- *A New Earth* by Eckhart Tolle
- *Total Meditation* by Deepak Chopra
- *Breaking the Habit of Being Yourself* by Dr. Joe Dispenza
- *The Big Leap* by Gay Hendricks
- *A Course in Miracles Made Easy* by Alan Cohen
- *Becoming Supernatural* by Dr. Joe Dispenza
- *The Surrender Experiment* by Michael Singer
- *The Untethered Soul* by Michael Singer
- *It Didn't Start With You* by Mark Wolynn
- *The Monk Who Sold His Ferrari* by Robin Sharma
- *Journey of Souls* by Michael Newton, Ph.D.
- *The Tao of Success* by Derek Lin
- *The Tao of Daily Life* by Derek Lin
- *Autobiography of a Yogi* by Paramahansa Yogananda
- *Taoist Parables for Young Hearts* by Karthik Muthaiyan
- *Ask and It Is Given* by Esther and Jerry Hicks

There are SO MANY books, courses, teachers, philosophies and you may already be well-grounded in one or another. The point is that without some form of self-reflection, some form of at least attempting to understand who you are, how you think, why you act as you do, then all the money in the world can't fulfil you.

If you find the very idea of self-exploration difficult, one thing you might find useful to know is:

Humans have been engaging in self-exploration for centuries, if not millennia. For example, in Vedic, Buddhist, and Yogic teachings, there are four major goals in life: prosperity, pleasure, life purpose (or calling), and self-actualisation (or spiritual values).

So, the idea of gaining financial freedom (prosperity), time freedom (pleasure) and emotional freedom (life purpose and self-actualisation) is not new. However, it seems many, if not most people in modern society have forgotten or choose to ignore these essential concepts. They chase money but sacrifice their health. They get spiritual but remain financially strapped. There is a better way.

Our hope for you is that you experience the complete freedom triforce: Financial Freedom, Time Freedom, and Emotional Freedom.

Chapter 21

Access Denied

By the time our extended visa ran out in the Maldives, we hadn't seen our families for a year. We decided, once again, to attempt to get back to the UK. The problem was, the Maldives was still on the red list. We needed to find a green list country where we could stay long enough to clear border control once we arrived home.

Red, Amber, Green

We were watching the lists — trying to figure out the best way to get back to the UK. Which country could we use? It was all very last minute, waiting to see what the Government would do.

At the time, anyone arriving from a red list country had to stay in a quarantine hotel for 10 days (11 nights). Anyone arriving from a country on the amber list had to self-isolate for 10 days. And if you arrived from a green list country you were free to walk off the plane and go about your business. I'd be damned if I was going to spend good money in staying in a Government 'Quarantine Hotel' on our arrival back to the UK if we went there directly from a red list country. As far as I was concerned, the quarantine hotel was my nemesis at that time!

It turned out that from the green list, there was just ONE country in the world that would let us in from the Maldives (without a vaccination) which was also on the UK's green list. We could go there for 10 days and then get back to the UK without a quarantine hotel.

So I said, "Great. Dave, we're heading to... Slovenia!"

Slovenia... or NOT?!

We had 24 hours from this discovery to get covid tests, flights and a hotel organised. There were no direct flights to Ljubljana, the capital of Slovenia, so we decided to get on a flight that had a change in Zurich (the alternative was Singapore! Which just seemed a crazy distance out of the way!). Our flight arrived at 6:00 p.m. into Switzerland and we had an overnight stay as our ongoing flight wasn't until 10:00 a.m. the next day.

We were fine with an overnight. Zurich Airport actually has a hotel — the Transit Hotel — located in the airport. BONUS! We could get a good night's sleep without even having to leave the terminal!

After disembarking the flight from the Maldives, we walked up to Passport Control to see if we could go to the hotel just the other side of security.

"Can we go to that hotel, there?"

The Swiss border guard asked three questions, "Do you have a vaccine? Where are you flying from? And where are you flying to?"

"We're coming from the Maldives, we're flying to Ljubljana, and no we don't have a vaccine."

"No."

Chin up, as they say, right? So, I replied "Oh, that's a shame. No worries, we'll just go and sleep in the departures lounge."

"No."

Oooookaaaay.... "Can you please give me more words?"

"No, you are not going to Slovenia."

I'm thinking what is this guy on about. OF COURSE we're going to Slovenia! S-L-O-V-E-N-I-A. I did the classic foreigner thing of talking louder to try and get my point across, waiting for the point to land...

"No, really, I get that we can't go to the hotel, but we are going to Slovenia. We have a flight booked on Swiss Air for Ljubljana, tomorrow at 10:00 a.m."

The Swiss border guard gave a little shake of his head and looked me straight in the eyes. "No, you're not."

This wasn't going well. Clearly he knew something I didn't know but he wasn't being very forthcoming.

So, I asked "So, why we aren't going to Slovenia?"

The Zurich Interchange

Dave and I hadn't been vaccinated yet.

We couldn't get it done in the Maldives. Instead, we literally had to come back to the UK for that. You may remember all the rules around vaccinations. No country was giving away their vaccines. Every country was focused on vaccinating their own population first. You had to get vaccinated in your own country even if you were travelling to or staying in another country.

So when we got to Zurich, we weren't allowed into Switzerland. They wouldn't let us in because we weren't vaccinated. Funnily enough, if the UK had still been in the EU at the time, they would have let us in. But, because of Brexit, they wouldn't. But as far as we were concerned that should have been fine, because we were only transiting through the airport so we weren't actually going into Switzerland.

"Sorry, you're not allowed past this barrier, because once you get past this barrier you are in Switzerland. And, unfortunately, your flight to Slovenia departs from a gate in another part of the airport. That part of the airport is also in Switzerland. So, you're not allowed to pass this barrier and you won't be able to board that flight, because you can't come into Switzerland."

Dave and I looked at each other, slightly confused. We'd booked our flights on Swiss Air. Surely, the airline should have known this?

"This is just a transfer to another country where we are allowed in. Can't we just go through and go straight to the departure gate?"

"No, you can't come into Switzerland. You're not allowed to go to Slovenia. In fact, you're not allowed anywhere in the Schengen Area! Don't worry, however, we'll just put you on a flight to the UK."

Wait. What?! NOOOO! That was the last thing we wanted; the whole point was to avoid the 10 day quarantine hotel! My nemesis! We had to think fast.

"What about going someplace else?"

The Swiss border guard was looking a little impatient by this time (it was Saturday evening!). "You can either go to the UK or go back to the Maldives. It is your choice. Either go back to your original destination or back to your home country. It is fine... We will pay for your flight on the grounds of refused entry."

So, they would have paid for our flight but... quarantine hotel?! NO.

What about the Maldives? We didn't want to go back. Don't get me wrong, it was great. After three months on the beach, and our amazing new morning routine, we were SO chilled out! But, we were kind of done with that. Thinking on our feet we started considering other options.

"What if we were happy to go somewhere else? We've also got residency in South Africa, could we go there?"

A bit bemused, he said, "Yes, that should be alright."

Of course, this wasn't solving our issue in any way because South Africa was still on the red list. We quickly checked other possible destinations and there was just one. It wasn't as good because it was on the amber list, but at least it was a step in the right direction.

"What about Dubai, can we go there instead?"

The guys at border control looked at us like we were mad. You could almost see the wheels turning: *Who are these people?!*

With a slightly bemused look on his face he replied, "You have five minutes to book a flight."

Dubai (and the CBD Scare)

"Fine. Thank you."

Of course they had taken our passports, so we didn't have our passport information to hand. Then we started thinking about the rules around PCR tests. At the time, you had to take a PCR (swab) test within 72 hours of getting on your plane, and then provide evidence of a negative test to be allowed to board.

Easy, right? Except we'd just travelled from the Maldives. So, now we're doing time zone calculations in our heads, trying to figure out if we were still valid for travel. Meanwhile, the Swiss border guards were breathing down our necks telling us we had five minutes to book the flight.

But again, after three months of chilling, we were not going to have our mood ruined by an overly stern Swiss policeman. In fact we were both laughing about it at the time, simply amazed at the twists and turns that life was throwing our way.

It actually took 10 minutes, but we managed to book a flight to Dubai that departed the next day, two hours before our PCR test became invalid. The Swiss border guard was happy to have us out of his hair, gave us back our passports and sent us back into the terminal.

By this time, we were hungry. With the new optimistic version of myself now in charge, I said, "Don't worry, Dave, there will be somewhere to eat. We'll have a nice evening in the airport."

Little did we know...

We found the only food place open in the international departures lounge at Zurich Airport — good old trusty Prêt. But they were about to close, and there was only ONE singular chicken salad left. Literally nothing else. That was it! So, our 'nice' dinner ended up being a salad and a plastic bottle of wine. Not to worry, the next day we were off to Dubai!

The airport was basically empty, so we made ourselves a nice little bed on the benches. At least we didn't have to curl up on the floor somewhere. I decided to Facetime with my mum because she was expecting us to call from Slovenia the next day.

"Hi, Mum! Guess what? We're actually NOT going to Slovenia. We're now going to Dubai!"

After our Facetime I was lying on my 'bed' on the bench in Zurich Airport trying to get my head around where I'm going and what the heck I'm doing. Then something my Mum had said started setting off alarm bells in my head.

When I told her about going to Dubai, Mum had said,

"Dubai? Oh, right. Well, I hope you haven't got any drugs in your luggage... or they'll put you in prison for 25 years!"

I went into Incognito mode on Google, thinking somebody might be watching. (After all, I'm in the airport, we've just been denied entry and hurriedly booked a flight to another country. Better safe than sorry, right?)

It turns out Dubai are quite strict about which substances can enter their country.

Uh, oh.

"Dave... you know that CBD oil in our luggage?"

"Yes."

"It is against the law to travel into Dubai with CBD oil."

"Oh C**p!"

Now, to understand what a mess this all was...

Our luggage had originally been checked through to Slovenia. When we booked the flight to Dubai, they'd pulled our luggage off the plane, but it was still waiting in transit. In other words, it was in Switzerland... you know, the Switzerland that had just denied us entry! So, we couldn't just grab the CBD oil out of the luggage and toss it in the bin. However, we knew we had to find a way to get access because the alternative was to potentially get arrested upon arrival in Dubai!

So the next morning before our flight, we went to the flight information desk and, after explaining our predicament, asked how we could access our luggage.

"I'm not sure, you'll need to speak to the security guys to see if they know".

So off we went to the security guys, spent another five minutes explaining, to which they responded...

"We can't get it for you, you'll have to talk to the luggage handlers — there's a phone over there you can use to contact them."

So we got on the phone to go through the rigmarole of explaining once again, to which they responded...

"I'm afraid we can't bring it to you, you'll need to speak to the border control to see if they can help."

Nooooooo! Not border control again! Those guys are going to roll their eyes when they see us again... But off we traipsed to border control and explained our issue for a fourth time.

"Sorry to say that I can't help you, you'll need to speak to the Airport Police". So he called a policeman to who we went through our fifth rendition of our story.

"Can we please get access to our luggage? We're going to Dubai and we have CBD oil in our luggage and we don't want to go to prison."

He was not friendly. I explained the situation, from our arrival to the moment we realised we could get into trouble. He didn't say "No problem, wait here and someone will bring your luggage."

Instead, the first thing out of the Swiss policeman's mouth was: "Is there any THC in it?"

In case you don't know, THC (tetrahydrocannabinol) is the chemical in cannabis that makes you high. CBD (cannabidiol) is also made from the cannabis plant but it doesn't get you high — it isn't psychoactive. So, the Swiss border guard asked because THC is illegal in Switzerland but CBD oil is not.

Of course, we said, "No, it's just CBD oil."

"Yes, we'll help you get your luggage..." Hoorah "...but we are going to have to test it. If it has more than 0.1% THC in it, we will have to arrest you." He laid it on thick, trying to scare us, even going so far as to threaten us with a lifetime ban from the Schengen Area. I got the strong impression that he felt even CBD should be illegal!

Eventually, they escorted us through the Swiss part of the airport (that we weren't legally allowed to be in) so that we could retrieve our luggage from the transit holding area. He tested the CBD oil, and there was NO THC in it... So we weren't barred from the Schengen zone for life, and we also weren't put in prison on arrival to Dubai. Successes all round! Needless to say, by this time I was thinking *Get me out of Switzerland. Please!*

Me at Zurich Airport with my best 'get me out of this country NOW' face.

Eventually, we got on our flight to Dubai. But I have to say, it's the first time ever that I've wondered if I'd get into a country as we came in to land. I genuinely had no idea, but also didn't actually mind.

Why? Because we were so chilled, and we'd just had three months of emotional letting go. So literally nothing was stressing us out, not even the prospect of prison! (Crazy, right?!)

The good news was, Dubai welcomed us with open arms. We even got collected from the airport (with only seven hours' notice) by some friends (thank you Sid & Kritika!) we'd made in the Maldives.

It was amazing.

The whole experience was such a CRAZY situation, but it leads perfectly to an important lesson.

Freedom Formula:
Adventure Is Better Than Stress

Prior to everything we'd been through that year...

The mad dash to escape England...

The red list and the decision to go from South Africa to the Maldives...

Getting an extended visa to stay for three months and work on ourselves...

I would have been SO stressed out over the drama in Zurich. Going through what we went through, I would have felt AWFUL and WORRIED. But we didn't even mind that it was happening.

Actually, it was just FUN! I didn't mind that I wasn't going to Slovenia. And I didn't care that I might not get into Dubai. It just felt like it was all part of the adventure of life. Dave was the same and it was such a BIG SHIFT for both of us.

Life is an Adventure

Through all of this we remained 100% upbeat and good-natured. We saw the whole thing as an adventure. No stress! For me, especially, this was a completely new experience. It was, quite literally, a new version of myself.

More importantly, this was the version of ourselves that we wanted to bring into the business! We wanted to be able to take on the challenges of growing our property business, and instead of getting stressed out as we always had done, we wanted to find it fun! And now we had just proved that was possible.

It might not be easy for you to begin — and persevere — in the quest for Emotional Freedom. It certainly wasn't easy for us. But every second we spent working on ourselves was WORTH IT!

I realised, after all the crazy things that had happened over the course of a year, that my PERSPECTIVE, the way I thought about these experiences, had a direct bearing on whether I felt stressed AND on my longer-term health.

Easier said than done, I know. But you CAN start today.

Chapter 22

2022 Déjà Vu

In 2022, a deal we'd been working on since our time in the Maldives was coming to a conclusion. Everything about how the deal would work had been agreed with the bank, and the agreement was integral to the project's success. Then, it happened. The now infamous...

Liz Truss Mini-Budget!

As you know, it wreaked havoc on most of the UK economy, including the property market. For us, as with all property people, it was massively detrimental. The day before the mini-budget, the Bank of England had raised interest rates by half a percent. So, we already knew our refinance was likely to cost more. What we could not foresee was the swift backlash the mini-budget would cause on the entire mortgage market.

As the pound dropped to an all-time low against the dollar, the Bank of England stepped in to buy bonds and prop up pension funds. Suddenly, banks started to withdraw mortgage products from the market. Unsure of just how bad things might get, they chose to wait for clarity about future bank rates.

So, after months of satisfying various questions, our lender decided to go back on everything that had ALREADY been AGREED!

11th Hour Rug Pull

The bank's decision destroyed the deal. Completely took down the plans for it. Crushed it.

It was a very similar situation to what had happened in 2018, when we'd tried to refinance the three properties in Margate...

- The bank said they would do one thing...
- Dragged us along for months (each month eating into the profitability and viability of the deal)...
- And then did something COMPLETELY out of alignment with what had been agreed!!

It cost us tens of thousands of pounds. Yet, somehow, it was different this time...

Evolution of a Refinance

Remember how frustrated and stressed I was when faced with the 2018 refinance?[1]

In 2018, we had fought back — complaining and insisting on a meeting with 'the powers that be'. We'd bashed our way through every obstacle to get our way. We wouldn't let anything stop us, no matter what, no way, we WOULD get the promised offer.

Except, THAT had proved to be one ingredient in the recipe for cortisol spikes and stress-induced depressive breakdowns. No thanks.

In 2022, it was different. Somehow, there was a little more space between us and the problem. We had been through so much, done all that great travelling, meditating, working on ourselves while still growing the business, that we simply accepted it.

For the first time, we just said, "This is the way it is, and it is outside of our control."

---

1. See Ch. 12: The Mortgage Offer and Down Val Debacle

Deals Dropped

We had a couple of other similar deals, blocks of flats, going through purchase at the same time, but with the rates getting to double where they were before, we decided to let them all go. Cancelled entirely because it didn't feel right – surrendering, rather than fighting, for the first time ever. It felt like the right thing to do... but that still didn't mean that it was easy to let go. It really felt like we were failing, and that did NOT feel good.

These were deals that would have brought in tens of thousands of pounds over the next 6-12 months. Instead... Boom. Gone, just like that. Our cashflow forecasts had all been done on the basis of these deals proceeding to completion. Our team plans had been made off the back of these cashflow forecasts. Very quickly the picture was looking very different.

The Veil of Perception

So in summary, that mini-budget was not exactly great for us! It seemed bad (really bad), but by this point we'd realised that so many things we perceived as 'bad' in the past had turned out to be positive in the end. So, despite the fact we didn't know how this related to the current situation, we decided not to fight.

Instead, we made a conscious decision to surrender and see where this seemingly bad turn of events took us. In the end, the deal we'd been working on since agreeing it from the Maldives, turned out OK.

It wasn't as profitable as we planned, but we found alternative ways to move forward. Whereas before we wouldn't have seen how to proceed, stuck in 'stressed out' mode, now we chose a different response. We got to 'everything turned out OK in the end' with a LOT less stress!

From a business perspective, our new way of perceiving things meant that we were able to look at the situation with far more clarity. Which, in turn, allowed us to make necessary business pivots quickly. We had to let some team members go on the basis so many anticipated deals weren't moving forwards.

This was the right thing to do from a business point of view, but from a personal perspective it was not what I wanted. They were friends and people I thought were brilliant and that I cared about a lot. To be honest, in the past I just wouldn't have been able to get past how I felt personally. I would have seen it as my personal responsibility to find a way to push through and probably would not have made that very tough decision. Having to let good people go really makes you face your fears of failure head on, and I just wouldn't have had the courage to do it a few years before. It was definitely personal growth, but it felt s—t!

Surrender Feels... Bad?

However, just because it didn't feel right to proceed with deals...

And just because we'd created enough space to make tough decisions without all the stress...

And the fact that we'd changed our perspective almost entirely from what it had been...

Does not mean it felt GOOD to choose this very different path!

In all honesty, this new approach of 'surrender' did not feel good! It is almost like surrender creates a gap between feeling bad about yourself and feeling good. And in that gap there is this other layer of the psyche.

I definitely didn't feel as bad in myself as I did in 2018. Instead, I felt... empty. A sense of apathy. Almost like a boat floating on the water with no destination. It felt like I'd lost some of my passion and zest for life... everything just felt a bit more 'grey'.

This was a conundrum. A new puzzle that needed solving because without the fight burning within me, I really didn't know who 'I' was anymore. I just knew I didn't feel like me.

The Grey Feeling of Indifference

So, whilst in 2022 we began to surrender and stopped struggling, we were still feeling a lot of frustration. How could this be 'me' when it wasn't? The person I had become was VERY different to the person who started this journey nine years before. And, somehow, I instinctively knew that even the person I had become would change and evolve and grow to get to where

I truly wanted to go... Emotional Freedom. But that would require letting EVEN MORE of 'me' go.

When you completely let go of something that you've held dear — even if that thing was harmful to you — there is a sense of loss, of grief. It is human nature. It is also an obstacle we must overcome. Wise seekers of truth from many cultures recognised this thousands of years ago and everyone from psychotherapists to self-help gurus see it today.

Today, you might hear someone say, "You have to get rid of the old to make room for the new." Or, "to reach THIS goal, you have to give up THAT behaviour." It's really a simple concept, right? Except applying it to your life and business can be a little more complex. Anything BUT easy!

In hindsight, that 'grey feeling of indifference' was a stepping-stone towards having the ability to feel great no matter what is happening. So whilst I wasn't enjoying that piece of 'grey emptiness' that was opening up inside me, it did start to have a use. It turned out that this little bit of empty space would mean that in the moment between something happening in life and starting to feel a negative reaction to it inside, there would start to be this very quick moment of reflection... is this a helpful reaction? Is this how I want to respond? There opened up an awareness of CHOICE, to choose a different way to respond from a different level of perspective. It really felt like a new kind of Freedom coming in... and we laser focused on it.

Sometimes it was harder and I could feel the grip of negativity wanting to drag me down. The small amount of space and questioning myself in the moment wasn't enough. This was the same for Dave too. When this happened, we started responding to each other differently than before.

Rather than trying to 'make the other person feel better' (in effect taking responsibility for their reaction), we would start (lovingly) telling the other one to... "Go and meditate.". Dave helped me continue to focus on taking personal responsibility for my reactions, he wouldn't entertain the idea that the situation was to blame for how I was feeling. And I did the same for him in his moments when the old self wanted to grab back control and make him self-sabotage.

We'd stop what we were doing. We'd cancel meetings if we had to! And we'd go and find a quiet corner, put in our headphones with some calming music on (like the 'Endel' app, or Solfeggio frequencies on Spotify). We'd breathe, centre ourselves, and find within ourselves the new perspective on the situation that we WANTED to choose... and move ourselves towards it.

It wasn't perfect, and sometimes it might have only been 50% good... but it was a consistent commitment and focus to changing ourselves (rather than the external world)... and ultimately changing our lives in the process!

As long as we are growing and spending time out of our comfort zone, we are always going to have to confront our fears. By fears, I mean the parts of ourselves that we've done a great job of hiding from... but that we can no longer hide from if we want to keep moving forwards and growing.

To achieve Emotional Freedom, you may have to let go of what you've always held onto as your core drivers and motivators, and get through the same grey feeling of indifference that we went through for a time. Perhaps you will ask questions of yourself...

- *What is the point of this?*
- *Why does this even matter?*
- *Is this all there is?*
- *Is my property business giving me everything I've ever wanted?*
- *Do I even need this property business to get what I want?*

Right now, as you read this, you may be in a completely different place in your journey. Maybe you are still working on Financial Freedom. Maybe you already have enough income from property but you are working 12-18 hours, six days a week. Or, maybe you have Time and Financial Freedom but it feels empty...

As you read the next chapter, keep this lesson of letting go in mind.

Chapter 23

To Transform Your Life, Transform Yourself

In Japan, there is a tradition of repairing broken pottery with a mixture of lacquer and gold, silver, or platinum dust. It is called kintsugi (golden joinery) or kintsukuroi (golden repair).

If you've ever seen a bowl or teapot repaired in this manner, you know it is absolutely stunning. To make the repairs, each piece of pottery is carefully laid out to determine how it fits back together. Gaps — places where fine chips or larger pieces are missing — are noted. The craftsman then uses the lacquer and gold mixture to painstakingly, slowly, with reverence for the pottery, re-assemble it. Piece by loving piece. Gaps and imperfections are filled in until the vessel is once again whole.

The end result is... more.

Yes, it is a useful vessel, worthy of its original purpose. It is art, an object to behold and admire. It is whole again, but now it has a meaningful history. The breakage, the cracks, the imperfections have all been filled with gold, so the pottery is now more beautiful than when it was new. Perhaps most importantly, it is unique, never to be repeated in exactly the same way.

There is a philosophy behind kintsugi. When a piece of pottery such as a teapot breaks, the break is considered beautiful, meaningful, and part of the object rather than something to disguise and hide away. What we in the

West might consider ugly is looked upon as inspirational. It raises questions, inspires ideas, and highlights the beauty in broken things.

But it goes deeper, yet.

Kintsugi embraces imperfection and flaws, highlighting them, raising them to the surface, to the forefront of perception. *Kintsugi celebrates imperfection and flaws.*

This chapter is about flaws. Broken or missing parts. It is about a reality we all know, but few embrace and even fewer celebrate.

Unworthy

2022 felt like failure to me. We had been through SO much and come SO FAR. Yet, when I looked in the mirror, I found it difficult to recognise the person looking back at me. Success — the idea of success — had driven me for the past decade, if not my entire life. When things went well, I felt 'whole' or 'good' (or, at least *thought* I felt good).

But when things didn't go my way or the business faced challenges, I felt unsuccessful. When I wasn't achieving the things that I set out to do, I felt deeply unworthy. Not good enough. And it made me realise how important 'success' had become to me.

This breakdown — of things not always working the way we wanted (or expected) in the business — caused me to question, deeply, who I was. It caused me to wonder why, if things weren't 'going to plan', I felt unworthy. And that led to a painful breaking of the 'way things have always been'.

That sense of breaking, painful as it was, created space. With space, new joy and energy can come in.

The Subtle Art of Choosing

I had always been attached to striving and achieving. In fact, I identified with striving and achieving. It wasn't just something I did, it was who I was. This realisation — that I didn't know who I was *without* striving and achieving — made space for me to choose. I could, intentionally, decide to become someone new rather than just carrying on as who I'd always been.

I had made the decision to become financially free and made choices to achieve it. Then I decided time freedom was the goal and made choices to get there. When we started working on ourselves whilst in South Africa in 2021, we really weren't sure what that looked like. We didn't know the outcome. We hadn't really identified the Emotional Freedom part of the equation. We only knew that we didn't want that underlying stress and anxiety we felt.

Now, I realised that all along I'd had the power to choose. Like the vessel repaired by kintsugi, I could be remade, putting the pieces back together and filling the spaces with joy and new energy, highlighting my own flaws and imperfections to become a new, more beautiful and unique version of me.

I finally made the decision to start choosing HOW I WANT TO FEEL first. This became my goal, over and above financial or material targets. I came to realise that I can choose my own emotions. I don't have to achieve things in the external world to feel good. In fact, that 'need' to achieve in the external world will always feel futile in the end, because even once achieved, it is always replaced by a 'need' for the next thing.

Mind you, there is a difference between choosing something and avoiding something.

Energy Liberation

I once heard someone say that getting into the psyche is like peeling an onion. First, you peel away the brown, almost crusty layers. Then, you get a firm layer that looks better, but is already transitioning to skin. Then, you peel that away and find something that looks beautiful but brings tears when you cut into it. Finally, you dice it, add a little oil to a pan and cook the onion slowly to get something sweet, something nutritious, something that brings flavour to everything in life.

Trying to push negative feelings away as soon as you experience them is not letting go. Yet, it is a mistake I made — and a mistake I see some of our mentees make. As painful as it is, you have to do the work of peeling away the layers, dicing the onion, and confronting the negative feelings (tears) that come up.[1] In 2022, I had to confront the very negative feelings that came up. It was just like peeling that onion, going deeper, layer by layer, trying to get to the good part, only to find it brought more tears and more work. But, in doing so, I finally started to let go and transform myself.

One of the biggest shifts through this is how I feel about myself and react when I'm struggling. The first difference is that I now see the fact that negative emotions are showing up as a good thing, as an opportunity to let go of something (Michael Singers' book, *The Untethered Soul* is great at describing this in more detail). I no longer push the negative feeling away... instead I lean into it. I allow the scary feeling to express itself in the biggest way it can, and then from that place it's amazing, but it dissipates. You think if you let yourself feel negative emotions, that you'll get stuck in it and never come out of it again, but in fact, the opposite is true.

As part of this letting go process, I don't allow my mind to get involved. I've realised, it always wants to blame someone, something or some situation for the fact I have a negative feeling... but I just don't buy into it anymore. I allow those thoughts to pass, and instead just focus on the feeling instead.

Then as the negative feeling starts to let go, I focus on coming back to a relaxed, peaceful, centred state. Sometimes this is as far as I go, but if I feel I can, I'll focus on going even further and choosing a more positive emotion to bring in instead. That to me now is what FOCUSING on FREEDOM means. The ability to CHOOSE. To choose how I feel and to understand that the external world and situations are not responsible. I am.

The amazing thing is that the energy I had been putting into pushing those negative feelings down or away was liberated. I could now envision a future with genuine freedom and choice. Ironically, it was the freedom I'd really been chasing this whole time. My entire journey as a property investor had come full circle.

---

1. It is important to note that many people seek professional help to confront negative emotions or overcome obstacles. There is no shame in this and both Dave and I have worked with a therapist, as well as with Stacey Rochelle on natural health, and with Dominic Beecheno and other coaches you have read about in this book. There is no honour in trying to tell yourself "I got this" if you don't. Remember, the top performers in EVERY field of endeavour, have coaches. Many work with mental health professionals. And it is a process.

Freedom Formula:
The Power to Transform Yourself

We don't have to let the world control our emotions; we have the power to choose. We can choose to Let Go of anything that comes up that we don't want. When we Let Go it allows us to focus 100% of our energy towards taking positive action rather than having it sucked into the vacuum of negativity.

Have you heard the one about the woman who, after 10 years of hard work and graft, was an overnight success?

2022 taught us so many things, but mostly it made us realise that we were transforming ourselves. The painful business pivots, the feelings — first of indifference and then of freedom and kintsugi-like rebuilding — started to open us up to feeling free, truly free, for the first time.

As 2023 went along, we started to be able to move past challenges in a very different way. In our business, we suddenly had a sense of *Boom, on to the next plans.* The business was growing again and everything was OK. We didn't allow stress to affect us in the same way anymore. We were now dealing with challenges in an entirely different way. Regardless of what was happening in our business, in the property industry, or in the economy, WE WERE OK.

But the realisation went one step further — and this is the lesson:

We had been holding ourselves back.

It was us... Not the economy... Not the bank... Not vendors, COVID, or the Government... Not the industry or anything else... WE had been holding us back, keeping us from being happy.

We had been holding ourselves back the entire journey!

After nine years on this journey we knew that we were never going to get to the freedom we wanted until we changed ourselves. Otherwise, we would always have that feeling of anxiety, stress, weightiness, regardless of how 'successful' we were... feeling like something else needs to change or get better or get done *or else I'm not going to be happy.*

Whereas in the past I was skeptical about personal development and changing myself (because I'd got where I'd got by being who I was?!), now I knew that personal transformation is essential. It is key to the entire equation.

If you want to transform your life...

If you want a better life...

If you want to be happy...

If you want freedom...

You've got to transform yourself FIRST.

Because THAT is the route to changing everything else. Everything.

Chapter 24

Opening Up to the Unexpected

Even though there was a lot of inner turmoil going on in 2022, there were still some truly beautiful moments travelling.

The contrast between trying to figure things out and actually living is part of the process of self-exploration. Anyone (yes, anyone) can develop a meditation practice. But after those 30 minutes a day, how do you bring it into the rest of your life?

After the Inner Turmoil, the Beautiful Moments

In the early part of 2022, we spent eight weeks touring the Garden Route in South Africa. Mossel Bay to Storms River along the coast with botanical gardens, secluded beaches, Wilderness National Park, and Plettenburg Bay. It is one of the most beautiful 'road trip' adventures you can imagine.

January 2022, the Garden Route, South Africa

We followed our South African adventure with six weeks of skiing in the French Alps. There wasn't much of a plan for what to do next. We talked about Portugal or perhaps Greece. Eventually, we decided to go to Portugal to play golf for the spring.

So, we started booking Airbnbs near golf courses but... something about it just didn't feel right. To this day I have no idea why. The idea seemed great, who wouldn't want to spend 4 weeks playing golf on the sunny Algarve, but I just wasn't really feeling it.

We were on a chair lift after a ski run when this idea just came to me out of left field. So, I floated it to see where it might land with Dave...

Chairlift Decision Making in Three Easy Steps

"Dave, maybe it's not... Maybe Portugal isn't it. What do you reckon about... getting a motorhome instead?

In the past, Dave would have contemplated this idea, thrashed it around a while, come up with a list of pros and cons. Detail Dave, right? Well, at this point, after all the meditation and focus on personal development, Dave was getting quicker with decision making. He was learning to trust in what life presented and in his instincts.

He took about 5 seconds to contemplate it before saying, "I think it could actually be a good idea."

Within a matter of HOURS, we'd decided. We're GETTING a motorhome. Within a matter of DAYS we'd found a motor home, spoken to the dealership, secured it, flown back to the UK and agreed to BUY said motor home.

This was a complete left field idea that had come out of nowhere. Just like that, EVERYTHING changed. Suddenly, we were travelling around in a friggin' motorhome!

We were meant to be in Portugal, playing golf, and staying in Airbnbs. Instead, with our new motor home, we travelled around Europe, staying at amazing vineyards, and wild camping. I'd never heard of wild camping before. You find beautiful places and just go and park your van there — for free.

Staying in all these nice places, all I could think was *This is INCREDIBLE!*

October 2022, parked up next to the sea in Greece

And it just came out of absolutely NOWHERE! However, it didn't come without... challenges!

MoHo Winter

Spending Winter in a motorhome is... one hell of an adventure! We went from 35°C in Croatia in August, to -20°C in Austria in January! All in a van!

MoHo Winter! Staying next to the ski lift in Hintertux, Austria, January 2023. Temperature: -20°C!

The winter, in particular, was a big learning curve. We've got great heating in the van — it uses gas for heating when we're off grid. Our first night in Hintertux we were confused about why we had woken up freezing cold with frozen taps. It turned out we'd burned through half a bottle of gas in 24 hours and therefore the heating had turned itself off! Normally, a gas bottle lasts four to six weeks in the summer. At Hintertux, at -20°C, we burnt through 22 kg of gas in... three days!

Dave kept saying, "Stop turning up the heating, you just need to put a jumper on, Jackie!"

We loved finding new, exciting, off grid locations to camp. Imagine, just you, your partner, and an epic view... mountains... lakes... fresh air... it was stunning. And we never quite knew what the next thing 'not panning out like we expected' would be... and we found a way to love the adventure of things 'going wrong'.

Once, Dave had to get under the van to de-ice a wheel that was frozen solid. Then we realised that the whole car park area was a complete sheet of ice! Somehow, we had to figure out a way to turn the van around on this sheet of ice. Did I mention that we had meetings that day? We'd left ourselves one hour before the meetings began, thinking that would be more than enough to get to our next destination. We ended up using up the entire hour just trying to get out of the car park. The solution... using bark from nearby trees to make a track so we could drive over the ice (my idea I might add... Dave was sceptical it would work).

Another time our exhaust started to fall off and scrape along the ground. I can't tell you how many Fiat garages we visited to solve various issues. Here's another picture of Dave in January 2023, just before a quarterly investor meeting... under the van again. He was defrosting the wastewater pipe with a HAIR DRYER! (Notice he was still smiling...)

Dave under the MoHo defrosting the water tank with a hair dyer!

It was like everything that could go wrong, went wrong. But we were LAUGHING! We weren't even bothered about it. It didn't matter — it was all part of an adventure and we were enjoying it.

Motorhome or Pizza Van?

Mostly things DID NOT go wrong in the van though... We have had some AMAZING experiences in the motorhome. It has completely changed our perspective about SO many things.

For example, we have a pizza oven that we carry around with us. You can make pizza anywhere, in any weather. Yes, even at -20°C, Dave was outside making pizzas! He's become quite the pizza chef.

Dave making stuffed crust pizza in -20°C weather for my 33rd Birthday. Me, so ready to eat. (It was a GREAT pizza!)

We have a different perspective on space, too. How much space does one really need? We travelled through all seasons. Skis, jumpers, coats... everything needs space, right? But it truly is just a matter of perspective.

What many people may consider to be a negative has actually been a very positive experience for us. This lack of space has forced us to live with only the essentials that really matter to us. Getting rid of stuff that we would normally cling on to for no other reason than not wanting to throw things away.

Letting go of stuff is truly freeing! It feels like you've decluttered your brain, and it brings your focus to the things that really matter. We now love spending our time in a small space, because it brings simplicity to our lives. A simplicity that wouldn't be there if we were still able to surround ourselves with clutter. It's also strengthened our relationship, as being in such close proximity all the time has helped us to become more patient with each other and aware of each other's needs. In fact, it's been such a freeing and positive experience for us that I now feel like everyone would benefit from spending 6-12 months in a motorhome!

The World Is Our Oyster

In 2023, we were once again featured in *Your Property Network* magazine because of our adventurous lifestyle.[1] Everything seemed to be happening, it was all starting to flow a lot more than ever before. It seemed as if it was all too easy. For us, that felt a little weird. Challenges were coming up, but we didn't mind. There's a lesson in this about what many people call your 'comfort zone'.

There are times when what feels comfortable isn't actually good. Like the body's addiction to cortisol when its purpose is to help us deal with danger. Or those times in life when you don't take action because you *think* you might fail, or you *think* someone close to you might ridicule you. For us, we'd been so used to these big challenges, that when things started to flow, to get good, it weirdly took us out of our comfort zone. We just weren't used to things being easy, so we were out of our comfort zone.

1. The article, titled "The World Is Our Oyster: Reaping the Financial Freedom Rewards", along with the other resources mentioned throughout this book, can be found at: www.property-strategy.com/focus

The Try Harder Illusion

All these little challenges? Now we think of them as adventures. And each adventure gave us an opportunity to learn.

Problems Are Opportunities

This might sound strange, but the motorhome has been an amazing teacher for us.

So many things go wrong that you have, for all practical purposes, two choices:

1. Get upset, frustrated, angry (or any other negative emotion you can imagine), and eventually give up. Or...
2. You can roll with it, enjoy it, learn better how to let go with each and every small disaster.

This brings up another very important lesson. This applies to life, to your property business, to almost everything.

Believing that you can somehow control everything if you TRY hard enough is...

A Very Costly Illusion

I lived this illusion for a long time. *Try harder, Jackie. If you only try harder, you'll get this under control... Everything will work out if you just TRY HARDER!*

You have control over one thing - this moment. That's it. Nothing more. Don't take this the wrong way — I'm not saying you should stop taking action or that actions don't have consequences and sometimes those consequences are off in the future.

No. This is about what you can actually control... which is only one thing... how you think and respond in the fleeting moment known as NOW. Right now. What you do at this moment, how you think at this moment... the action you take in this moment. If you truly want to be free (and I know you do because you've made it this far!) then you MUST learn to take action and then LET GO. Do not hold onto any stress in-between action and outcome.

Dom Was Right

Turns out Dom was right, back in 2020, when he told us at our retreat dinner to 'set goals and let them go'.

The irony is, we mentor dozens of property investors now and we see this all the time. It's as if our clients reflect back to us what we've been through. It makes us realise just how much we held on to stress unnecessarily. And we see clients do the same — until we help them see the futility, the illusion, of trying to 'be in control'.

You've got to make the plan and then let go. Whatever it is you are doing in property — it doesn't matter what the business model is. It doesn't matter the economic environment. It doesn't matter what courses or trainings you've done. Make the plan. Let it go. Get on with acting in the now.

Remember, letting go doesn't mean don't take action or not caring.

If this seems challenging, consider this: No plan will EVER go exactly how you expect. Life really doesn't work that way. Business doesn't work that way. There are always tweaks, pivots, iterations.

Freedom Formula: Revel in the Unexpected

Our MoHo lifestyle has taught us to FIND THE JOY in the unexpected. None of the 'problems' we experienced were planned. But it was FUN! The fact that it wasn't planned made it MORE FUN because our perspective had changed so much compared to how we looked at situations before. Before, when something went wrong, we blamed it, or we blamed ourselves, and we didn't feel good about it.

Life is an adventure. Business is an adventure. Turn everything into an adventure. Let go of HOW it pans out. Don't cling to situations or circumstances because something even better, or easier, might be coming along.

When you get this — an emotional letting go — you will revel in the unexpected. You will know that you can just take action to resolve what's going on and then let go of the stress related to it. There's really no need to worry about ANY of it. And what happens if you can manage to do this? Then I've found that you unleash a massive reservoir of energy, happiness, headspace, time, problem solving genius, and a reservoir of personal Freedom that was previously hidden behind your own stress and worry.

Chapter 25

The Beginning of the End of Striving & Pushing

As we moved into 2023, our travel adventures were really just flowing. Little things were going 'wrong' all over the place, but we didn't mind. Things that would have stressed us out before, didn't phase us. We started to understand that the stressed state isn't how we (humans) are supposed to live.

Seeing this new perspective play out in our travels, we started finding ways to bring that into our work. How could we create this same sense of freedom in our business?

Time to Start Allowing & Flowing

When something went wrong, we sometimes still had a reaction that we didn't want. We still had emotional triggers and hard-wired neurological pathways to contend with. The difference was that we were able to catch ourselves SO much sooner. This level of awareness had developed over the previous two years as we investigated what was going on inside.

Understand that it takes time — none of this kind of work is instant. That said, you can start today by changing (or even creating) your internal dialogue.

It starts with two self-referential questions:

1. Why am I stressed about this?
2. How can I reframe this situation to see it from a different perspective, as an adventure, or something fun, or something to learn from?

As you ask these questions — and contemplate the answers — you start to practise not having that stress reaction. This, in turn, slowly but surely rewires the brain's neurology and reconditions the body's reactions. Then you practise flowing your way through whatever situation, circumstance, or business activity is on your plate right now.

Evolved

Through this process of creating an in-the-moment practice, I realised that I had been ADDICTED to having a stressed feeling whenever I worked. And it wasn't helpful any longer. Better yet, I could start to train myself to have more fun... be more flowing... feel more enjoyment in work. Even in the things I didn't want to do. I realised that the more fun it all was, the more it all flowed.

Work was starting to get EASY AND FUN and I was more excited than EVER about what I was doing. (As I write, this is still true!) Now, Dave and I love what we're doing! We have really evolved.

Now, we...

No Longer Strive for the End Result

This brings so much more JOY to work! We set goals and then let them go. We focus on how we can ENJOY doing our work. The result is that MORE great stuff is happening for us... much EASIER than it ever has before.

This led to us looking at 2023 as *the beginning of the end of striving and pushing*.

Maybe I'm still striving. But I'm 90% good. Choosing to end striving and pushing opened us up to allowing and flowing. We've stopped judging things so much. If something happens that we didn't plan, so be it. We've stopped being so attached to the way things *should* be. Instead, we enjoy whatever comes up 90% of the time.

Evolved Vision

Our Vision with Tomes Homes had been to have 100 homes in 100 locations across the UK. In our minds, the plan was to just replicate what we were doing in Thanet. So we thought we would analyse and choose a new area to start investing in. Then, we would build an 'on the ground' team for each new area just like we had in Thanet.

As we let go of striving and stopped being fixated on how we were going to achieve this plan, something magical started to happen. It was as if all the pieces of a puzzle started to come together, and we saw the big picture in a new way.

A Beautiful Synergy

We first started mentoring property investors in 2016 and we've been running our Deal Maker Accelerator (DMA) programme since 2020. However, after the 'busy idiots chasing our tails' experiences we had early on, we'd always kept the investing and mentoring totally separate. They were two completely different businesses.

In DMA, we had (and continue to have) a small but amazing group of property business owners — many of whom we've worked with for three-plus years. Most had faced challenges similar to ours and have come out the other side with stronger businesses. In 2023, there was this unexpected but very welcome shift.

That year we started to bring the personal development revelations we'd had into our mentorship. We saw so many examples of business transformation with our DMA clients that it was incredible. As we started to dig into what was behind everyone's unprecedented business progress, in almost every case it was due to personal transformation.

On the surface, it looked like the business had been transformed overnight. But the personal transformation was something they'd been working on for three months, six months, nine months... And what they achieved in comparison to what they'd done before was amazing.

We have this great bird's eye view of our mentees. We get to see exactly who they are and how that impacts their business success. It became clear to us that the results they had achieved in business were a direct reflection of:

- How they were feeling — not on the surface, but at a deeper level.
- What they were doing in life, i.e., how they went about their day-to-day, their habits.
- Their state of being, whether that be frustration or joy, self-doubt or belief, anxiety or flow, trying to control every outcome or letting go.

It was incredible to see that mirrored so wonderfully. They were following our playbook for growing a business and funnily enough... they were investing all across the UK. Suddenly we saw something we'd never been able to see before...

What if we could bring these two sides of the business together? What if those 100 different locations could happen thanks to a network of partners whom we've mentored for years? Partners whose businesses we know both outside and in? Partners whom we've seen deal with challenges...

In other words...

The Perfect Joint Venture Partners

Suddenly, it was so clear. We could add value to our investors by having the ability to deploy many millions more in capital than when investing only in our own projects. And we could do this in a far more diverse selection of areas. At the same time, we could add value to our advanced mentoring clients by giving them access to funding for their deals. That would save them from having to deal as much with banks.

All of this happened with ease. It wasn't contrived or planned out for months or years in advance. It was us being open to ideas and possibilities because we were no longer striving and pushing for a preconceived notion of how it would all play out. We were clear on the vision, but then we were just going with the flow for how we would arrive there.

The Podcast Phenomenon

The same thing happened when we decided to launch a podcast. For years people in the property industry had been telling me I should. For years, both myself and Dave had wholeheartedly resisted. There was no plan for that happening. It just presented itself, it happened, and it was easy and fun! Once we'd made the decision to do it, within months we'd launched our top 10 charting *Property Lifestyle Mastery* podcast with EASE. That would NEVER have happened a few years ago.

Here's another example...

We always loved the idea of running a retreat overseas. But it always just seemed too difficult to work out how to make it happen, so we had resisted it.

After our DMA mentees started requesting it, we surrendered. And, as with the podcast, it came together in a way that we would NEVER have expected. The Retreat was a purely personal development retreat... Oh my days! If you had told me that a few years ago, I would NEVER have thought that's what I would be doing. We were just following what felt right, and being guided by how we could serve others to the best of our ability. I will never forget the sight of a retreat full of property investors... all scattered around the swimming pool with their headphones in... going through a half hour meditation.

It was one of the most fulfilling things we'd done in our lives because the inner perspective shifts led to the most incredible shifts in the businesses. In the couple of months after the retreat, we saw more finance raised and deals agreed than in the rest of the year leading up to that point! We were helping our mentees to break through barriers in a much easier way. It takes a lot of courage to be able to look deep within yourself for a solution and to accept that it is YOU that is holding yourself back – but doing that with others made it easier. We really went through something together that weekend – I will never forget it. It was a springboard into a whole new direction for Dave, Dom and me... doing deals and raising finance through personal transformation.

In fact, it was so transformational that we decided we had to start running retreats like this for other people in property who were not part of our

DMA programme, because we could see how much it would change peoples' businesses, lives and ultimately have a positive impact on the whole property industry. And so our new Property Business Breakthrough Retreat was born!

The first ever Property Business Breakthrough Retreat in Italy 2023

The Real Easy

2023 was the most insane year for BRILLIANT stuff happening. It was also incredible to step back and examine how far I'd come.

This 'let go and let it flow' version of me... this is not who I had ever been. I've always been the person who's got a plan. *She's striving for it... She's pushing for it... She's going for it and won't let anything get in the way...*

I stopped striving and started to try and enjoy every day, no matter what it involved. So, it wasn't just a year of business transformation for our DMA mentees — it was a year of complete business transformation for me... because I was having more fun!

Freedom Formula:
Re-Form the Habits You Live By

How, then, do you get to the point of letting go and letting it flow?

It's one thing to recognise there's a problem, but it's another thing to be able to change habits. We are doing more than we've ever done before and having the most fun we've ever had — all because we've started to **let go of the habitual addiction to worry and fear**.

So, what about those pesky habits?

Certain habits serve us well, like brushing our teeth or effortlessly tying our shoes. Other habits... well, not so much. *Do I really need that extra glass of wine? Or that bag of crisps?* Importantly, the brain doesn't 'care' whether the habit is positive or negative! That's because it created the habit in the first place to conserve energy.

I spoke in Chapter 19 about Joe Dispenza's *Breaking the Habit of Being Yourself* and described the exact neurological processes behind our habits and addictions. Well, in *The Power of Habit: Why We Do What We Do, and How to Change*, author Charles Duhigg describes how the brain creates habits via a three-step loop: the cue, the routine, and the reward. The reason this is important is because once a habit is formed, the brain stops working as hard. It is as if, at a conscious level, it turns off — freeing the brain for other, top-of-mind, tasks. So, to stop or change a habit you have to consciously and deliberately break some part of the three-step loop.[1]

It turns out that it doesn't matter what type of habit we are trying to break. Only one step in the loop needs to be broken and changed.

The lesson at the end of chapter 18 gives you a six-step method for how to do this. Briefly, here are the six steps again:

1. Charles Duhigg, (2012) *The Power of Habit: Why We Do What We Do and How to Change* (London: William Heinemann), ch. 1, p. 20

1. Get Calm and Centred.
2. Practise a Positive Emotion,
3. Imagine a Negative Emotional Situation.
4. Detach from the Emotion.
5. Accept and Let Go.
6. Replace with a Better Emotion.

Here's a high-level view of where that fits into the three-step habit loop:

The six steps above all relate to changing how you respond (your routine) to the cue that triggers the habit. The first step on the habit loop — the cue — is out of your control. So, to change the habit, you focus on changing the routine.

That downval, the builder letting you down, the bank not coming through, whatever it is — is out of your control. The routine — the second step in the habit loop — is what you CAN control. The six steps listed above (explained in more detail at the end of chapter 18) are a powerful way to change the second step in the habit loop.

This concept – breaking the routine whilst the cue and the reward stay the same – has influenced the treatment of hundreds of mental and physical health issues from alcoholism to obsessive-compulsive disorders and weight loss.[2] It is also used to train for high-level performance tasks — think athletes, musicians, dancers — anything where habit is key to success. (Arguably, this applies to everything in business and life as well.)

Now that you know, it is time to start recognising the cue, detaching from the emotion, and choosing your new response.

I realise now that this is how we could have always been doing it, because life is much easier when you are flowing with it rather than fighting against it.

Resources

If you want to retreat from your life and business for a few days to breakthrough the biggest blockage that's holding you back from raising finance so you can do more deals, then you can check out the details here www.property-strategy.com/pbb

Chapter 26

The Freedom of the Big 2023 Refinance

So far, we've discussed most of the major challenges we've faced over the years. You've heard a lot about the s— that we've been through, the ways we've dealt with it, and the lessons learnt. I've shared our evolution and how we shifted from always being stressed to discovering we could control our internal response. This shift came into stark relief in our big refinance of 2023.

This is a story about what can happen if you allow yourself to evolve and to meet familiar challenges with a different response.

The Beach Rise Refinance

In the introduction to this book you read, briefly, about Beach Rise — a project that was finally ready to refinance in 2023. It was a big refinance. We were expecting about £1 million in investor finance to come out of it and wanted it to happen quickly and painlessly.

Dave got the valuer in to view Beach Rise in May. We expected two weeks for the valuation to come back and another month for the mortgage offers. The reason we were optimistic about the time frame was because the refinance was happening with our current bank. They already held the first charge on the property and had been happy to lend against it when we purchased it. So now, all they needed to do was release capital. We figured four weeks should do it.

When the valuation came back in late May or early June, it was brilliant, even better than expected. We thought *This is AMAZING, we're sorted!*

It was the first time we *hadn't* braced ourselves for a down valuation. We'd had so many downvals in our time — more than actually makes sense. With our new state of mind, we thought maybe it was actually our fear of getting a bad valuation that had been somehow manifesting this. So we decided it was time to try something new! We decided we wouldn't worry about it. We decided it was going to be a GREAT valuation. Anytime any negative thoughts or ideas started to creep in, we would shift our perspective and think *if we get a downval, it doesn't matter, we'll figure it out... and for some reason, it will work out for the best.* In a way that gives me goosebumps when I think about it... it ended up being the BEST valuation that we'd ever had.

Of course getting the valuation back is just the next step – you then require a mortgage offer. In July, 4-6 weeks after the valuation coming back... we still did not have a mortgage offer to sign. Then August came... still no mortgage offer. Going back to 2018, we would have been so stressed out. We'd have been ruminating on it, waking up early worrying about it, talking to each other about it all the time. Continually reinforcing the stress and rationalising it as necessary.

This time, there was none of that. We just carried on with life. We carried on enjoying our lives. Knowing that happiness was NOW – NOT on the other side of the refinance.

We still took actions to move things forward — chasing up and nudging the process along. The difference, though, was that the chasing up was done without the stress and anxiety... it turns out those feelings DON'T HELP. You can do all of the same actions, but with a completely different volition behind it. It was exactly the same issue we'd had in 2018 — an issue that had caused soooo much stress.[1] However, due to all the work we'd done on ourselves, proactively retraining our neurological responses and focusing on improving our internal reactions, we now had a very different response.

---

1. See Ch. 12: The Mortgage Offer and Downval Debacle

Instead of being fraught with frustration, we were now able to find joy and happiness regardless of the business challenges. Now that's what I call true Freedom!

We finally got our mortgage offer in September after three months. It was WAY less than we'd anticipated. The bank had promised us 75% loan to value (LTV). Instead, it offered us 67% LTV. Dave and I looked at each other when it came in. There was a moment of silence between us... in that silence was a moment of CHOICE. Choose to be angry, frustrated and to fight? No. It's like we were having a telepathic conversation in the blink of an eye... and we both smiled, and started laughing...

"It's still going to release a great amount of money", I said to Dave.

"Agreed! Let's not fight this, this is clearly how it's meant to go," said Dave. And on we went with our lives.

It took another three weeks for the funds to be released. Whereas I had expected the refinance to be done in July, it wasn't finalised until the end of September. The entire refinance took six months rather than our estimated 6-8 weeks. We did everything we could to move it along, but we did not put our lives on hold and destroy our health in the process.

The fact we'd approached this with a whole different openness and energy meant that when the funds did finally land we weren't exhausted and worn out by the process... instead we were RARING to go to get the funds invested, and invested in a completely new way that we would never have spotted had we'd been stuck in the grip of stress.

What had changed?

WE had changed. It was the moment when we FINALLY were able to look at it in a new way.

This is the exact same thing that has happened to us so many times before. But this time, we're still happy. And because of that, business is still flying. It is amazing. We are DIFFERENT PEOPLE.

Beach Rise By the Numbers

I think this is the best deal we've done to date. Here are the numbers:

Purchase Price	£1,400,000
Purchase Costs	£75,000
Refurb	£450,000
Finance Costs	£114,000
End Gross Development Value (GDV)	£2,840,000
Project Profit	**£835,000**
Total Investment Required	£1,032,000
JV Partner Investment	£600,000
Cash Left In (67% LTV)	£99,000
Ongoing Cashflow (per Calendar Month)	£2,400
Return on Capital Employed (ROCE) after Refinance	29%

Notice the profit? Remember when I first started networking and getting distracted by shiny pennies? When I met the 'coolest ever dude' doing commercial conversions, who wouldn't get out of bed for less than £500k profit on a deal?

Well... we managed it! £835,000 profit with a total return on investment of... roughly 83%. WOOHOO! And no commercial conversion required!

If we'd got the 75% LTV mortgage, this would have been an all money out deal with cash left over. In the end, the 67% LTV meant leaving £99,000 in, but it earns £2,400 a month which translates to 29% return per annum.

As you can see, our JV partner put in £600,000. When the project went over budget, rather than tap him for more capital, we brought the rest in on loans from other investors. So, our JV partner made a profit of £400,000 on their £600,000 investment.

Truly Believing

By 2023, we had both *Surrendered.* No longer did we feel the frustration, the worry, and the anxiety. Full transparency: there are moments when these feelings try to come up, but we are able to call upon our practice and choose a different response. This is all possible due to a mindset change.

When life challenges us now, we think things like:

- *Things always work out for the best (we just can't see it yet).*
- *This is how it is meant to be.*
- *None of it really matters anyway because success in business is NOT the point of life.*
- *My happiness is more important than worrying about this.*

But just thinking these things on the surface is not enough. When Dave and I think this way, we truly believe it. This was a big challenge for me in the past, but it is KEY. Does this sound almost TOO easy... too simple... clichéd even? After all, you can't really 'think your way to riches and freedom'... can you?

I'm not suggesting you drop everything you are doing and try to wish riches and freedom into existence. However, every circumstance, every challenge, every obstacle is an opportunity for you to think in a way that brings it closer or pushes it further away. To make it clearer, let's look at what happened in 2022 in the light of this new mindset...

Bad Thing or Good Thing?

Remember the Liz Truss Budget and our sense of déjà vu with the bank? We hadn't responded with total stress like back in 2018. By 2022, we'd figured out how to create a little space. But if you remember, it didn't really feel good. We still had this underlying feeling that what happened was a bad thing. And even though we eventually came to realise that 'this is beyond our control', what came out of that was a grey feeling of indifference.

With the benefit of hindsight and more clarity about how to change our emotional response, we came to realise that the deals we'd had to pull out of would have been EXTREMELY challenging in the wake of interest rate hikes. Whereas we had perceived the bank to be messing us around as a 'bad thing' (having led to us pulling out of two deals) ... in reality it was a really GOOD THING.

As it turns out, the events of 2022 were exactly what was meant to happen! And had it turned out like we had planned, we could have been in a much worse position.

Freedom Formula: Freedom Is a State of Mind, Not an End Goal

In 2021, when we sat in those deck chairs in Cape Town with a feeling of unexplained background anxiety, this was what we had to learn.

Freedom had ALWAYS been available to us. Even back when I worked in market research and wanted to be able to not have to ask for permission to go on annual leave. I chose to feel caged, anxious, held back, like the world was against me being free, but I could have chosen to feel this feeling of freedom back then.

That doesn't mean you should give up on property or building a business. You should go for Financial Freedom and Time Freedom. You still want to go on the journey. But understand that the FEELING of freedom is available now. If you're waiting for an end result to feel the feeling of freedom, you're waiting to be disappointed. You might get to the end result, but it won't give you the *feeling* of freedom. The feeling is a choice. We actually CREATE the feeling of freedom.

You Can Practise Feeling Free

You can go into a meditation and ask yourself *what does freedom feel like?* And you can bring up that feeling now and practise feeling it. And when you do this, you will literally be changing the wiring in your brain to allow you to feel it more easily next time.

My wish — our wish — for you is that you go out there and make Financial Freedom and Time Freedom a reality. But PLEASE make it more fun than Dave and I made the eight or nine years leading up to this realisation!

It could have flowed. It could have been more enjoyable. More magic could have presented itself had we allowed it to happen instead of being attached to stress. We allowed stress instead of allowing freedom. We thought the world was making us feel it. We THOUGHT it was downvals, builders, banks, structural engineers, valuers, the economy, building control... or whatever else.

No. It was our choice, and that choice made the journey less enjoyable and much harder. And had we been less tenacious, it could easily have jeopardised our ability to achieve the financial and time freedom that we wanted.

What we are experiencing now is joy. We enjoy every day, and business is better (yes, we're actually getting better results!). More opportunities present themselves and we are better able to take advantage of them. Things flex and pivot easier. Everything flows better and we grow faster.

I think this mindset, this FREEDOM mindset, is one of the biggest factors that could have halved the time it took us to get where we are now. If we had managed to approach everything like this from day one... GAME. CHANGER. We would have been quicker to rebound, quicker to pivot, quicker to do new things and without chasing so many shiny pennies...

Other people would have responded to us better. Potential investors, banks, vendors, builders, our team...

A final thought about freedom as a state of mind:

You CAN be happy. You can choose to be happy doing almost anything for a living. Choose to be happy AND do awesome things! Choose Freedom.

Chapter 27

'You' Won't Be the One Getting There

In November 2023, we were back in the UK for a celebration event to mark 10 years since deciding to start investing in property. When we were back, we had a meal with some of our JV partners: Sid, Arti and Mo.

Reflecting on the fact that 10 years had passed, Arti asked us, "Where do you guys see yourselves 10 years from now?!"

This simple question had the most profound effect on us. I've always been a planner. I've always had goals. Together, Dave and I have been strategic planners — almost to a fault when we were trying to do too many things in 2015 and 2016. Of course you plan the future, right? You've got your goals, you've got your vision, and then you take massive action, right?

It was so strange because we were stumped. I couldn't believe it but I didn't want to answer the question. This was such a weird experience for me. I used to LOVE being asked that question... I'd always have such great answers!

I'm Not the Same Person You Knew Back Then

We were silent for a few moments. I think we were having an internal moment of our old selves wanting to wade in and berate us for not having planned more... *You SHOULD know the answer to this.*

Finally, Dave broke the silence.

"The problem is, 10 years ago I couldn't have ever imagined where I'd be now. And the reason is because I'm a different person now than I was then."

Think about that for a moment. Whatever it is you want, whatever it is you are trying to achieve, when you get there... YOU will NOT be the same person you are now. This is one of the great truths in life that many people overlook. It isn't something they teach you in school.

Teachers don't say "Hey, go out there and fail because that will help you become a different person in 10 years and that person will be better, more incredible, and will have more to offer to the world."

That's not what society teaches us even though the people creating the most impact have usually all failed, multiple times. Or gone through some transformational experience. But the reality is, over time, every day is a transformational experience. You become a different person every single day than you were the day before.

People's lives rarely 'go to plan'. What if you focus so much on executing your 'plan' that you close yourself off to other opportunities?

If I choose where I'm going to be in 10 years, I could be limiting myself. That version of me I'm seeing will be a limited version of what I could really become *because THIS me, the NOW me, can't even imagine what is possible.* The person I'm becoming will be able to do things that I can't even imagine right now — just the same as the me from 10 years ago couldn't see what I have become and how much I've grown.

We realised that night that even saying, "This is where I see myself in 10 years..." in many ways creates a self-limiting image. We weren't willing to limit ourselves anymore.

Vision Quest

To be clear, I am NOT saying you visualisation isn't great. Nor am I saying you not to have dreams or goals. The concept of a vision board is fantastic. Having things to aim towards is human nature, it pushes us to grow and progress.

But that night, sitting at dinner, with the question hanging in the air… there was a sudden shift. When Dave answered, it just became so clear. I knew exactly what he meant, and I felt the same. I'd never felt that before, but he was right.

I won't be the one getting to that point 10 years from now. I will be someone different, with more experience, more joy, probably having made more mistakes and faced more challenges. It will be a different version of me. Nowadays, if I were to say "in 10 years' time I see myself here"… I would REALLY STRUGGLE with it. Because looking at where I am now and where I've come from, it just feels like it's going to limit me.

Instead, I now find it best to set myself a goal, or an idea for where I'm headed, but then I just Let it Go rather than working to try and make it a reality. I then Focus on enjoying the moment now. And we consciously tell ourselves to find joy any time it isn't happening.

Life's Little Shortcuts

Head in the direction of the goals you've set yourself, but know that another route could open up at any time. You might not be able to see those routes if you've got too much tunnel vision on the goal. In my experience, this obsession with the goal means you miss the shortcuts because you are stuck in your old way of thinking. However, as you move towards your goals, you will be changing, you will be becoming a different person.

As you move towards your goals and become a different person, new routes will open up to you that weren't available to the old version of you. If you allow the new version of you to see — to become aware of — the potential routes, you will suddenly see the shortcuts. But if you are fixated on one path, one way, one route, you will miss them.

So it's that feeling, that sense and intention that, *as I evolve, as I grow, new options will become available. My job is to notice, to be aware.* When you do that, amazing things begin to happen.

Tunnel Vision

Whenever Dave and I talk about being open to new routes or shortcuts, two related questions inevitably come up.

1. How do you know if you are seeing a Shortcut, or being distracted by a 'shiny penny'?
2. Isn't it better to have tunnel vision, to block everything else out? What's the difference between being focused, and having tunnel vision?

Well, there's no perfect answer for either of these questions, but as a general rule of thumb I have found the following applies:

Shiny Penny Syndrome is usually a distraction towards an entirely different business model, or different methodology, where you don't know enough about it to realise how hard it's going to be. Whilst a **Shortcut** is usually a different way of doing something within the model you are already doing, and it often gets noticed with a shift of perspective rather than due to some brand new information.

A reminder that the solution for anyone who finds themselves getting sucked in to Shiny Penny Syndrome is to go back to your *Property Strategy Business Plan* and write that new idea down in the Future Ideas bank. It will still be there when you are ready. But unless it is truly a shortcut, it's probably a distraction to follow that path.

As for the second question...

Focus is the tenacity and willpower to keep your attention on the end goal regardless of challenges and distractions that come your way. Whereas tunnel vision is the blinkered vision that tends to arise when things become stressful, causing you to no longer be open to considering different options that may be available to you.

We've found that tunnel vision closes you off from potential opportunities. And we've observed the same with our mentees. Oftentimes, the tunnel vision approach comes when they face an obstacle or a challenge, then they get that cortisol spike, stress kicks in, and they put the blinders on because 'hell or high water, this MUST get done'.

In doing so, they tend to close down, and feel as if there aren't any solutions, meaning they fail to see other opportunities and avenues available to them. We did the same thing for years. Now, with this realisation that we are actually becoming different people as we move forward, it is much easier to take a step back, to meditate, to exercise, to take a deep breath, look around and become aware of options, opportunities, and alternatives. It is SO refreshing.

You might be thinking to yourself, "Jackie, what gives?"

Earlier in this book, I spoke about time blocking as a method to getting more done to create your ideal life.[1] I even told you to take yourself forward in time 10 years, to visualise your Ideal Lifestyle...

Wait. What? Was that a complete contradiction to what I've just told you to do!?

Let me be perfectly clear and re-iterate: having goals, a vision board, dreams are all GREAT. You want to imagine your Ideal Life in the future to help you start to build momentum and get you started on the right path. So, don't discount the exercise you completed after reading that chapter. (You did it, right? If not, DO IT!)

This is about understanding that as you head towards that Vision, you will always be changing. So when you get there — when you reach that time and place in 10 years' time — it won't be the same YOU and it won't look at all like you envision it today. Set the intention for that vision, and then be flexible enough to allow it to evolve as you evolve. And more importantly, know that when you can find JOY in the JOURNEY, the next 10 years will be much more fun... and it probably won't even take you 10 years to get there.

---

1. See Ch. 10: How Holiday Every Six Weeks FINALLY Happened

Chapter 28

Step Into the Magical Flow

Dave and I have been very tenacious in building our property business and we've worked hard. That said, up until we started actively and deliberately working on personal development in 2021, if problems came up, we bashed our way through.

In my meditations in the Summer of 2023, I started to become aware of how we had always tried *hard* to build our business and building the business had always been hard.

Stated another way: in trying so hard to build the business, we made it hard for ourselves.

In contrast, our amazing travels over the last few years have seemed to happen almost effortlessly. From being 'couped up' in the French Alps during the first COVID lockdown, to travelling along the coast of Italy, to our Cape Town escape and subsequent personal retreat in the Maldives... Even our crazy experience in Zurich and the Dubai diversion. Travel just flowed.

Looking back now it is clear to me that we had *allowed the travel to happen naturally*, always following what life presented, going with the flow and keeping flexible. In other words, we had followed...

The Path of Least Resistance

The idea of flow, of taking the path of least resistance, goes back thousands of years – it is one of the themes of the Tao Te Ching, which is said to be about 2500 years old. There is a related concept, also Taoist, called wu-wei, which means 'effortless action' or 'without exertion'. Our travel adventures seemed almost completely effortless, whilst business had always been the opposite: EXTREME effort and MAXIMUM exertion! But then, that's what stress will do to you.

In retrospect that's why planning out a holiday every six weeks had been so important, because I was finding work so tiring that I really needed a break every six weeks to be able to rebuild my energy to get back to 'pushing water uphill' when I went back to building the business.

The path of least resistance is always available, but most of us, most of the time, block it. At least when it comes to doing big things like growing a property business.

A brief but related aside here that you might find useful, or humorous:

A 2017 University College London study concluded that humans tend to make decisions and act based on what we think requires the least effort.[1] In other words, we may be 'hard wired' to do things the easy way, i.e., take the path of least resistance. Some psychologists have since cited this study as 'proof' that humans are lazy and will do anything to avoid hard work. For context it was a small study: 52 people in a controlled environment.

Well Life and business clearly do not happen in a laboratory setting!

Even if we are 'hard wired' to take the easy way, what we subsequently learn from school, society, our parents, our peers is NOTHING like this. We are taught to exert ourselves, to bash our way through, work hard, and overcome. We are taught to have... TENACITY!

1. Nobuhiro Hagura, Patrick Haggard, Jörn Diedrichsen (2017) Perceptual decisions are biased by the cost to act eLife 6:e18422. Available at: https://doi.org/10.7554/eLife.18422

The Balance Between Tenacity and...

> tenacity, n.
> The determination to continue what you are doing; firmness of purpose, persistence, obstinacy

Tenacity is all well and good. It takes tenacity to grow a property business. To do what it takes, for long enough, to reach a goal (even if it won't be 'you' that gets there) you will need firmness of purpose, persistence, and determination. You will need stamina, courage, and heroism. And intrepidity, pluckiness, doggedness, guts, and backbone... all synonyms of tenacity.

But we have found in our own business (and confirmed through working with mentees) that there MUST be a balance. Without balance, it is too easy to bash your head against the wall continuously, resulting in chronic stress or, having hit the wall one too many times, experience total breakdown.

And what of single-minded, pigheaded obstinacy? You could easily climb and climb and climb the ladder of success only to find you got the wrong ladder!

> "People may spend their whole lives climbing the ladder of success only to find, once they reach the top, that the ladder is leaning against the wrong wall."
>
> — Thomas Merton

Getting to the three freedoms we've discussed in this book ALWAYS comes back to a balance between tenacity and...

And, what?

Whilst writing this book, I once again looked up *tenacity* for an idea of what, exactly, to balance it with. What is the opposite of tenacity?

When I looked up antonyms, nothing seemed appropriate:

- Hesitation
- Indecision
- Timidity
- Fearfulness
- Weakness
- Impotence
- Timorousness (I actually looked this up! It means a lack of confidence.)

And the list goes on...

Not ONE of these inspires you to go out there and create an amazing business, let alone an amazing life! Is there NO positive word that appropriately balances with tenacity?!

Think about it...

In business (and in life), too much indecision stalls progress. It adds to anxiety and stress. Fearfulness leads to a lack of action. It might seem safe — after all, if you do nothing, you can't fail — but you won't learn and move towards your goals. If you have too much hesitation, too much fear, too much indecision or weakness you will never get ANYWHERE!

After a while, I realised that the English language doesn't actually have a positive opposite to tenacity!

Culturally Conditioned

That's when it dawned on me...

It's not the word, it's our culture. We are conditioned to believe that to NOT have tenacity is negative. Our culture doesn't allow us to choose an alternative to tenacity. That makes us miserable. It feels like you HAVE TO bash through, work hard and feel bad when things don't go to plan.

The answer came by going deeper with trying to understand tenacity. It turns out that a single, Proto-Indo-European root was

1. *Tenere:* which means "to hold, grasp", is the Latin source of tenacity.
2. *Tendere:* which means "to stretch", is the Latin source of the word tend, or "to look after".

What do we do with a garden? We tend it. The ability to tend a garden requires you 'to stretch' your imagination, to make continual small changes based on the season, the weather, the soil, the fauna and flora...

In other words, to be FLEXIBLE!

The balance I was looking for actually comes from the same root, but Western culture doesn't promote it as such. In our culture, you either have tenacity or you are weak. You act with determination or indecision; persistence or hesitation. That isn't the way life and business really work. At least not if you want the three freedoms.

I propose a new way to think about it: If you want to achieve Financial Freedom AND Time Freedom AND Emotional Freedom, you have to balance tenacity with flexibility. To achieve balance, you have to know *when* to be tenacious and when to be flexible. Which means you first have to understand when tenacity goes too far and turns into head bashing.

Tenacity is getting to a challenge and not giving up; head bashing is when you keep pushing down a path when there's an easier option available. So learn to recognise when tenacity ISN'T the answer.

Freedom Formula: Step Into the Magical Flow

Remember what Dom said to us in 2020?[2]

> "You have to set a goal, and then you have to let it go."

I was so SURE that he was wrong. *Hard grit got me here. Determination got*

2. See Ch. 13: From Cocky to Couped Up

me here. Tenacity got me here... I didn't get here by f——— letting it go! I got here by holding on to my dream with a firm grip and BREAKING DOWN WALLS.

Except all of that holding, attachment, perfectionist BS just slowed everything down. Now? I can confirm that Dom is, in fact, 100% correct. You do have to set your goals and LET THEM GO.

This is not to say that you won't have to DO something, to take action, to work hard. But once you've identified a state of flow, once you've learned to step into that state of flow, you are able to take action and do things from a place of enjoyment. It creates a feeling of satisfaction and fulfilment. And, it is more likely to get you an end result that you love.

Try this...

Know what you want — set the goal — and let it go. Then, start heading in the right direction whilst having as MUCH FUN AS POSSIBLE along the way! Enjoy the shortcuts that present themselves when, and where, you least expect. Allow life to help set the path for you. Allow the unexpected. Start to notice how easy things can be if you just let them. This is the way to step into the magical flow.

Chapter 29

Final Learning: We Created Our OWN Barriers

What if I told you that the obstacles, challenges, and barriers you face in your property business are all self-imposed? Some people might feel a little uncomfortable with this. Or unable to relate. We've been conditioned to believe that the problem is 'out there'... outside of us.

This journey Dave and I have been on has allowed us to focus inwards and shine a light on this area within ourselves. We've come to realise how much we truly held ourselves back through subconscious, self-limiting beliefs and self-talk. We held ourselves back based on how we perceived situations. We wasted time and energy and caused ourselves ill health.

I now know that all the barriers we encountered... were just barriers we created for ourselves.

If this makes you feel uncomfortable, you are not alone. I assure you, had someone tried to tell me this 10 years ago, I would have SCOFFED. Even five years ago I might not have believed it without a lot of convincing. But if I HAD been able to see it, to truly UNDERSTAND this, it would have saved me a lot of time, worry, and pain.

We all have subconscious beliefs, but most people lack awareness of how they affect us. They are, as Dom sometimes says, "unknown unknowns".

Yet, these beliefs hold us back from achieving our full potential. They are barriers keeping us all from stepping into your flow.

I refer to self-limiting beliefs here, but you could also call it self-sabotage. Either way, these beliefs are imprinted on us somewhere along the way, and they cause us to take (or avoid) specific actions. As opposed to the flow and flexibility of emotional freedom, self-limiting beliefs shackle us. When we try hard and try MORE to force business (and life) to work, it only serves to reinforce the binds that tie us. We actually strengthen the barrier by crashing into it because our conscious mind now has 'proof' that we are not smart enough, not capable enough, not hard working enough. Not Enough.

Stop. Take a deep breath. You ARE enough. You only need to learn how to flow.

It turns out that the ancient sages were right and their teachings are still 100% relevant today...

Nothing Compares to Water

Nothing is more flexible than water and, yet, it can overcome the greatest barriers. The following excerpt comes from the Tao Te Ching:

> *Nothing in the world is softer or weaker than water*
>
> *Yet nothing is better at overcoming the hard and strong*
>
> *This is because nothing can replace it*
>
> *That the weak overcomes the strong*
>
> *And the soft overcomes the hard*
>
> *Everybody in the world knows*
>
> *But cannot put into practice*[1]

1. Translation: Derek Lin, author of *The Tao of Success* and *The Tao of Daily Life*. This translation available at: https://taoism.net/tao-te-ching-online-translation/ (Accessed: 10 May 2024)

The ancient sages used water and its qualities as a metaphor for the way — for what I call stepping into the flow.

Water flows, therefore, flow like water. Rivers wind through hills, flowing around obstacles rather than trying to bash through them. And with time, the flow of a river can even erode those obstacles altogether without any effort. Therefore, flow like a river.

When you learn to do this, apparent obstacles start to disappear. It is a simple, but powerful route to achieving more in life with less effort. This is true in your property business, as well. It might seem vague, perhaps even mysterious, to think like this in relation to property. However, if you look around you at the truly happy and successful people, this is how they operate.

Our way of thinking — what we think is possible for us — comes first from conditioning. All you've learned, the culture you've been brought up in, your family, values, and beliefs, it is all imprinted on you. And it all has an impact on your view of the world.

You may have heard or read about money blueprints. The concept that those from a relatively wealthy background tend to carry on being relatively wealthy. They view money as 'not an issue' because they have a wealthy blueprint. They work hard and it comes to them. Compare that with someone from a very poor background. For them to make the psychological leap into wealth is very difficult simply because it is not their programming. Their programming is poverty.

The thing is, we can all name exceptions... people born into poverty who go on to create great wealth. History is filled with these stories, so you know it is possible. But how, if not through hard work, graft, grind, and head bashing?

With those 'rags to riches' stories there is always some experience or series of events that changes the way the individual thinks. Something happens to change how they perceive the world. They overcome the self-limiting beliefs that their personal history would normally dictate.

Are you aware of YOUR programming? What has your background imprinted on you?

For each of us, the imprinting is different. I was a perfectionist. Everything had to be perfect or it wasn't good enough. It still rises to the surface sometimes. But now that I recognise it, I can sit with it, feel it, and ask myself what is causing it. And, yes, I find after a bit of searching that I don't need to be perfect, and I AM enough exactly how I am.

Dave had developed different self-limiting beliefs. He studied music from a young age and went on to study viola and saxophone at the Royal College of Music in London. To reach that level requires an amazing amount of self-discipline. Hours a day in the practice room, grafting away at scales, working on technical proficiency, laying a foundation.

From this experience, he learned that to be successful, you have to work hard and that it is hard work. Dave believed that happiness would happen — the life he dreamt of — once he achieved all his goals.

He brought this same belief into the property business. He believed in delayed gratification, that he had to work hard now, all hours under the sun, and that happiness NOW wasn't necessary. He believed that once we had the big house, the car, the lifestyle... only THEN could we live the dream.

Now he realises that this is an illusion, self-sabotage, a self-limiting belief that was holding him back. Like me, he had created a barrier to his own happiness.

What It Means to Flow

I have a lot of conversations with mentees who question themselves: "Is this what I'm meant to be doing? I'm not sure, what do you think?"

The problem is, this is a very rational, logical way to work through the underlying feeling. I am of the opinion that you cannot *think* your way into the thing that you're meant to be doing. You've got to get underneath it and find a way to feel happier, to enjoy what you're doing right now.

I now believe that when you enjoy what you are doing, it actually leads you to your purpose. There's no need to go and seek it out because, ultimately, your purpose is not the thing that you are 'doing'. Your purpose is to FIND

JOY in what you are doing right now, even if it isn't what you would have chosen to do.

The funny thing is that as you find enjoyment in whatever you are doing right now, it actually leads you on a journey to a deeper purpose. You will suddenly find yourself doing something truly fulfilling that you would never have chosen for yourself. And you'll end up there so naturally, by a completely joyful surprise.

However, it is a process you must go THROUGH. You can't just tell yourself one day *Okay, I'm just going to change it now, I'm going to do it this other way right now.*

Why?

Because your hardwired, neurological responses trigger emotions and their connected chemicals. That then translates to habitual, addiction-based decisions and actions rather than conscious choices. And there is a constant stream of emotional triggers that you have to work your way through to get to the truth underneath it all.

My way of dealing with this now is to meditate every day. I look for the uncomfortable feeling, particularly on days where I'm doing things that I perceive to be work.

I have habitual feelings, naturally inside of me, reactions to the world as I've grown up. And those feelings make me want to behave in a certain way, to take certain actions. For me, one of those actions is planning. I have a chemical addiction to organising my to-do list, planning my diary, and making sure the team is doing what they are meant to be doing... a chemical addiction to order and control you might say!

Rather than letting the mind try to rationalise the feeling, and then let it control my actions, I instead focus on the feeling:

Let all that go and be aware of this feeling. Let it pass. Focus on the feeling. Let it come and then let it go.

Some days tears come during this process of letting go, and that's fine because once I've done this, I can approach work from a place of balance. Then I can actually choose what I want to do, rather than be railroaded into doing something by my emotions. And most importantly, I then enjoy what I'm doing. And working this way, amazing things happen almost effortlessly.

For me, this is what it means to learn to go with the FLOWWWWWW...

The Greatest Shortcut

It turns out that Freedom is available to all of us right now – we just have to choose to FOCUS on it. The incredible thing is you don't have to wait for Financial or Time Freedom to FEEL free.

As we work with our mentees each week, we see that those who embrace this deeper wisdom reach Financial and Time Freedom MUCH FASTER! They actually find it easier if they are already experiencing Emotional Freedom. When there are wobbles, which are inevitable from time to time, it is because they have created a barrier.

The first part of this book is about how to find your focus when investing in property. I have found that this focused approach simplifies the path to Time and Financial Freedom. But it also makes it easier to start working on Emotional Freedom.

When you FOCUS in your property business, emotional challenges become clear. But it goes deeper because focus gives you the headspace and time to work on those challenges.

I've found that EVERYONE, eventually, hits some kind of wall. They begin to encounter the same kinds of challenges over and over again. THIS is where the route into Emotional Freedom work lies. The more you focus, the more amplified and clear it will be. With practice, it becomes easier to identify problematic emotional responses.

For example, you may want to raise finance and work with investors, but you consistently do not take the required actions. You know what to do, and that taking action will lead you to where you want to go, but you don't do it. I now know that underneath that inaction and procrastination there is subconscious self-sabotage.

Rather than continuing to bash through or look to the external world to solve the problem, this is the time to focus. If you can have the courage to focus within YOURSELF, then THAT is the gateway to REAL freedom.

But like all worthy endeavours, it takes time and REPETITION. Which means you have to practise.

How?

Choose to focus on the feeling. To this day, it remains one of the most powerful meditation tools in my arsenal. If I start to feel the urge to change something in my life, I pause...

This is just a feeling. It is a habitual feeling and it comes from chemicals being released in my body.

If I sit and focus on that feeling, it starts to shift and move. When you come across an uncomfortable emotion that seems to be forcing you down a particular path, you have two choices:

1. Allow it to dictate your path (not recommended!)
2. Sit with it and really feel it through your body. Stare into it. Begin to ask: Where is this coming from? Why is this emotion trying to tell me what to do?

Dom sometimes calls this running towards fear.

> *"All fears are fears of feelings."*
>
> — Dominic Beecheno

Every fear creates discomfort inside: *Oh, no! You shouldn't do that. You don't want to do that.* It creates a physiological sensation that tries to guide you. Again, you have a choice. Your job is to sit with the feeling, to face it, to come out the other side into flow.

Feel Free Now

Do not wait to achieve Financial Freedom before you focus on making yourself truly free on the inside (like we did). Remove that limiting belief entirely.

It is all about HAPPINESS NOW. That is what will create the desired end result. To create success, focus on being happy now. Don't say "I don't need to be happy now" or "I don't need time to work on myself". Don't let those beliefs hold you back.

What is freedom, in the end? I would argue it's the freedom to choose HOW YOU FEEL about... well... everything! We built our entire company based on Financial Freedom, Time Freedom, and even Location Freedom. We fought for all that. But now I know that you could have all those freedoms and still have the same s—— feeling inside. Until you choose your feelings, you aren't free even if you have the other freedoms.

Do you have to go through the entire process to realise this? No. And yes, in a way. We've found that until our mentees experience Financial and Time Freedom, they often continue to think that those things must be the answer. So even though I can tell you it is not necessary, it really depends on your experiences, your background, and your imprinting.

I often hear people say, "once we solve this team issue, it will all feel great". Or "once that deal is over the line, I'll be sorted". Or "just let me get through this refinance and secure that deal and hit my cash flow goal, then all will be well".

It is human nature — we are always looking for the solution to our problems. But that problem you see in front of you? It is NOT THE PROBLEM! The problem is HOW YOU FEEL about the problem. To change the way you feel about the problem, turn it on its head.

When you get excited by the idea of solving the problem... when you enjoy every moment you put into overcoming it... it will no longer be a problem.

That is how you FOCUS your way to FREEDOM!

Conclusion and An Invitation

If what you've read in this book seems like a LOT to digest, I understand. What I've shared — the information and learnings about property, personal development and Finding Freedom — took us 10 years, thousands and thousands of hours (and air miles!), and many painful experiences to uncover. I wish I'd had something like this early in my property investing career. My sincere wish is that instead of feeling overwhelmed by everything in this book, that you find inspiration, see it as a shortcut, and begin stepping into your flow.

Everything in these pages is based on our own lived experience. I've only shared what we know works. Or, in the case of mistakes, what we know doesn't work.

I hope reading this book has been a beautiful, loving, heart-warming investment of your time. The resources I've mentioned in this book can be found at www.property-strategy.com/focus and I encourage you to take your time with them.

If you are wondering what to do first (or next), this is what I recommend:

1. **Complete your Property Strategy Business Plan.** It is a very good place to start. Financial Freedom is one third of our Freedom Formula. We've created the plan to help you get focused and cut

out unnecessary distractions. Just remember that it doesn't have to be perfect: good enough is good enough.

2. **Go through the exercises in the Freedom Formulas if you haven't already.** Find where the gaps are in your property business and begin to fill them in with the information provided.
3. **Start working on you and your feelings.** This is a lifelong process, so begin today. For me, meditation is key. I sincerely believe the entire planet should meditate! Go easy on yourself. Start simple.
4. **Seek mentorship.** We could not, and would not, be where we are today without the coaches we've worked with. Dom, in particular, has completely changed the way we think and do business. He is instrumental in what we teach and how our mentees continue to grow.

Our greatest joy, our purpose, is to help others Focus their way to Freedom. Yes, we are still doing deals, working with investors, and living the #holidayevery6weeks lifestyle. But seeing our mentees grow, not only as business owners but as PEOPLE, is absolute BLISS.

If you are interested in working with us:

- Check out our website: www.property-strategy.com
- Get weekly inspiration and insight from our podcast: www.property-strategy.com/podcast/

Also, I'd love to connect with you on social media...

Facebook: www.facebook.com/jackietomes1

Instagram: @tomesjackie

Thank you for spending time with me, and I hope we meet properly at some point in the future!

Jackie x

Resources

Throughout this book, I have mentioned various resources to help you Focus Your Way to Freedom. You can access all the resources (listed below) at: www.property-strategy.com/focus

Finances of Life

This simple spreadsheet is a great way to get your money management head on. Learn to focus on living with LESS in the short-term so you can have MORE in the long-term.

Investor Pipeline Mini-Course

Discover how to find deals and raise finance at the SAME TIME, without disappearing into a sea of overwhelm. Our process for getting deals funded seamlessly has helped hundreds of property investors grow their business with much less stress.

Property Strategy Business Plan

Our proprietary, one-page business plan was created specifically for property investors. Combining Business Strategy with Property Investing, the Property Strategy Business Plan will help you gain clarity about sourcing and acquisition, funding, delivery, financial management, and building a team. In turn, this will help you know what to prioritise in your property business at any given time, regardless of whether you are new or a seasoned investor.

Do More Deals Training Series

This training series is a ready-made strategy for building your monthly cashflow by working with investors to get property deals over the line. It will help you to refine your focus and take a more systemised approach, set clear expectations and prequalify investors, source more deals with confidence, and implement the entire strategy with ruthless efficiency to build your monthly cashflow.

Property Lifestyle Mastery Podcast

Property Lifestyle Mastery is where Dom, Dave, and I have open conversations about what it's like to build a property business that creates cashflow and Freedom. We share the highs, the lows, and all the lessons in creating the #holidayevery6weeks lifestyle. Food for your property investing soul!

Your Property Network Magazine

The UK's leading property magazine was instrumental in my early property business education and a great inspiration when I was getting started. We've been featured several times and I now contribute a monthly article. So be sure to subscribe after you've read The World Is Our Oyster!

Property Business Breakthrough Retreat

Breakthrough the biggest blockage that's holding you back from raising finance so you can do more deals at a stunning villa in the Italian countryside. Unplug from the day-today and transform yourself into the person who can raise £M's by clarifying your limiting beliefs, understanding where they come from and learning tools & techniques to overcome them so you can raise finance with confidence.

BONUS: Guided Meditations to Grow your Property Business

We talk a lot about meditation in this book. To help our mentees, we run weekly guided meditations sharing some of the techniques we use in our day-to-day mediations. I've pulled together a small selection of these that are about 15-minutes each so you can practise and experience first-hand the power of meditation when it comes to building your property business.

Biggest Thanks

My name may be the one on the front of this book, but it has truly been a team effort.

I would particularly like to thank David Wigram & Johanna Vivas – without the work of these amazing people, this book would not be here today. It has been a pure joy to make it all happen, and that is largely because it was not all on me. Thank you from the bottom of my heart for everything you have done for this project.

A massive thank-you to Dominic Beecheno, without him this book would have been half the size... he's an incredible inspiration and force for good.

To Sarah Burgess & Kathryn Simpson for their support and kindness in sharing their expertise and eagle eyes towards the end of the project.

To Lisa Oliver for giving so much time to provide valuable thought-through feedback on the book cover.

Also to so many others that provided support, feedback and inspiration along the creation of this book - I appreciate it all so very much.